macarthur in korea

the naked emperor

robert smith

simon and schuster
new york

SIMON AND SCHUSTER and colophon are trademarks of Simon & Schuster
Designed by Stanley S. Drate

Manufactured in the United States of America

10 9 8 7 6 5 4 3 2 1

Library of Congress Cataloging in Publication Data

Smith, Robert
     MacArthur in korea

     Bibliography: p.
     Includes index.
     1.MacArthur Douglas, 1880–1964.   2.Korea—
History—1945–1948.   3.Korean War, 1950–1953.
4.Generals—United States—Biography.   5.United
States.   Army—Biography.   I.Title.
E745.M3S57   959.9′03′0924 [B]   81-14522
ISBN 0-671-24062-5   AACR2

To my favorite cousins—
Marge and Joe Carey

contents

"But he has nothing on," said a little child.

FROM Hans Christian Andersen,
The Emperor's New Clothes

I
setting the stage

General Robert Eichelberger, a division and later on an army commander under Douglas MacArthur in the South Pacific during World War II, seldom mentioned Mac-Arthur by name in his letters to his wife. The code name he used for his superior was Sarah Bernhardt. And this nickname, many of his former colleagues agree, suits him far better than Caesar or Hannibal or Alexander the Great.

For, brilliant as MacArthur was in analyzing a military problem, putting his finger on its core and proposing a solution, and persuasive as he invariably proved in winning even adversaries to his point of view, he was concerned above everything else with the part he was playing—the part of a battlefield general, a spiritual leader, a selfless devotee of Duty and Honor, one of Nature's aristocrats, and a spellbinding orator. The fact that he was none of these things, and must have known in his deepest heart that he was not, corrupted his nature so completely that many of his colleagues and subordinates came to despise

him with a fury not even his death could extinguish. For
his feverish—often frantic and even puerile—efforts to
keep his image free from all blemish led him to lengths of
mendacity, self-aggrandizement, insubordination and hypocrisy that even some of his most assiduous sycophants
were hard put to ignore.

One thing MacArthur was not, however, was cowardly.
Despite the service scuttlebutt that nicknamed him Dugout Doug, MacArthur was far more than physically brave
in the face of enemy fire. He was reckless, rash, even fool-
hardy. When Japanese planes bombed Corregidor, Mac-
Arthur refused to seek cover inside the tunnel. Amid falling bombs and flying bomb fragments, making at least a
pretense of studying the enemy plane formations, Mac-
Arthur stood with his orderly at his side, while his orderly
tried to protect him partially by holding his own steel helmet over the general. (MacArthur would never wear a helmet, except for some formal photograph.) It was not that
MacArthur felt no fear. (The orderly said, according to
MacArthur biographers Clark Lee and Richard Henschel,
"I feel the general's knees shake.") Of course he was afraid.
Nor were his actions "suicidal," as some anonymous psy-
chiatrist whose opinion was solicited by a recent biographer described them. A better term would have been
counterphobic. MacArthur had learned to control his fears
by facing them every chance he got. When he came on
shore to view the progress of a landing, he often sought out
the spot where the fighting was hottest and stood exposed
to sniper fire while he studied a map, with his companions
all beseeching him to take cover. Once in the Philippines,
according to his ablest biographer, Dr. D. Clayton James,
MacArthur forged so far ahead of the invading forces that
he outstripped the "point" and came upon a still-warm
enemy campfire.

But his front-line appearances were rare and were, as he once explained to his wife, often necessary to bolster the morale of the troops. Ordinarily he held himself far from the action, although he liked his dispatches to indicate that he was practically on the firing line. He perhaps earned the title Dugout Doug when he studiously stayed clear of embattled Bataan, except for two brief visits. He always took care to shun lost causes.

Eventually, after escaping injury from shot and shell often enough, he came to believe quite seriously that he was protected by his luck—just as he came to believe (like a gambler who finds the cards running his way) that the gambles he took with the lives of thousands of other men were fated to succeed for no other reason than that it was impossible for him to lose. The few times in his life when he saw a gamble go wrong, he would shut himself away from questioners for hours, even days, or he would cast wildly about to find ways of dissociating himself from the disaster. Sometimes he simply pretended it was not a disaster at all, that he had planned it just that way. He could always count on his inner circle of admirers to sustain any excuses or explanations he might invent.

These were aspects of MacArthur's personality that revealed themselves throughout his career. But it was in Korea that they cost the nation most dearly and led finally to the dismissal he so richly deserved.

There is special irony in the fact that MacArthur should have met his ultimate personal disaster in Korea, for he seems almost instinctively to have avoided any deep involvement in that land, there certainly being no glory or preferment waiting there for anyone. And most of MacArthur's moves were made with a solid sense of where lay the best chance for advancement of his own career or enhancement of his own lot.

Yet, for the first two years of the occupation, Korea was MacArthur's responsibility, in civil as well as in military matters. While his job in Japan naturally absorbed his first attention, he surely might have kept himself better informed about the troubles that were brewing in the peninsula just one hundred miles from Japan across the Tsushima straits. MacArthur did require that the Commanding General of United States Forces in Korea report directly to him, even scolding him (through a subordinate) if he failed to relay information on some matter that might have involved embarrassment for the top brass. Most of the messages, however, were simply forwarded to the War Department without comment. And MacArthur ultimately seems to have swallowed, without question, the fairy tale that the South Korean Constabulary, the native "defense force" that was to man the border separating South Korea from the Communist North, was the "best little shooting army in Asia" (the words of Brigadier General W. R. Roberts, head of the Korean Military Advisory Group).

Nevertheless, MacArthur did interfere just often enough in Korea to help make war between North Korea and South Korea inevitable. The original choice of the War Department for Commanding General of United States Forces in Korea had been General Joseph Stilwell, a man thoroughly experienced in the Orient, without pretensions, and with sufficient political sophistication to have at least avoided some of the major blunders that marked the early months of our occupation. MacArthur, however, at the insistence of his good friend Chiang Kai-shek, vetoed this selection. With the Russians already having occupied Korea down to the 38th parallel (where they sat awaiting our arrival in accordance with the agreement on accepting surrender of the Japanese troops), there was pressure to get our own occupation forces into position quickly. The handiest forces were the two divisions of the XXIV Corps, under command of Major General John R. Hodge, then stationed in Okinawa, so it befell to John Hodge to take charge of our portion, a job for which he had no training and perhaps little taste.

Hodge has been pictured by left-wing commentators as a sort of born-on-the-farm bumpkin who did not know hay from straw when it came to anything other than farming or fighting. He was, however, besides being a brave soldier, a cultured gentleman, without affectations, basically friendly in nature and well-disposed toward the Korean people. But he was also a butcher in public relations, and what help he received from MacArthur aided him mostly in antagonizing the people he was supposed to lead to democracy.

The Basic Initial Directive supplied by the Joint Chiefs of Staff had been reduced at MacArthur's request to a mere set of guidelines. And MacArthur promptly ignored those guidelines in one most vital aspect. Paragraph 5f of the Appendix of the Directive contained these words: "Only in exceptional circumstances as determined by you, will any Japanese be allowed to hold any position of responsibility or influence (in Korea) ..." Whether MacArthur even read this charge, who knows? But he did immediately direct General Hodge to keep in power the Japanese Governor-General in Korea, with all his minions.

The Korean reaction, as almost anyone else might have expected, was one of foaming outrage—from left, right, and center—sounding all the way to Tokyo. MacArthur quickly ordered full speed astern. The harm was never undone, however, because in order to lower the volume of the protests it was necessary to dump every last one of the

Japanese bureaucrats, even those of low rank. And it took two months to accomplish that. Had the action been less high-handed—an immediate deposing of the hated top-rank Japanese and a winnowing out of the most offensive in lower echelons—it might have been possible to hold in place enough of the nine-to-five types to keep some sort of government functioning while transition was being made. This is how the Russians managed it.

As it was, there was turmoil and blunder right from the start. Hodge managed to stub his toe several times before he had finally settled himself in the seat of government and had appointed a military governor. When the main body of his troops was ready to disembark at Inchon, a noisy, untidy, disorderly but wildly happy crowd of Koreans had gathered to greet them so all could celebrate liberation together. But the Japanese police, there to keep order, fired into the crowd and Hodge's officers upheld them. To have permitted such a demonstration, they declared, would have "interfered with orderly debarkation."

Another mistake that Joe Stilwell probably would not have been guilty of can be laid to Hodge's lack of knowledge of Korean matters, the absence of any clear directive either from MacArthur or from the JCS, and Hodge's fear of burning his fingers by dealing with some so-called "government" that might even have been a group of Japanese conspirators in disguise. When his ship the *Catoctin* entered Inchon harbor he found awaiting him three men in a small boat, come to welcome him in the name of the Korean People's Republic. Hodge had never heard of the Korean People's Republic, nor of the men who were presenting themselves as its spokesmen. But these were the leaders of the actual Korean government-in-being, which had set up People's Committees in over a hundred cities and villages in Korea, north and south, and had pledged itself to moderation and to the maintenance of law and order. The leader of this left-leaning government was a sixty-two-year-old, but still athletic, handsome and widely popular, Social Democrat named Lyuh Woon-hyung, who had been assaulted by right-wing terrorists just before Hodge's arrival and was laid up for days thereafter. His brother, a man of more moderate political hue, Lyuh Woon-hung, and two other English-speaking officials of the "Republic" had set out in their frail craft well ahead of time, to be the first to greet the American commander. But Hodge kept them tossing there on the fearsome Inchon tides for three whole days, until their food was nearly gone. And even then they were permitted to state their business only to Hodge's underlings, not one of whom was ready to make any sense at all out of Korean politics.

Hodge also contrived, without intending it, to offend most of the plain citizens of Seoul by ensconcing himself in the palace used by the Japanese governor-general. He selected the place for no other reason than its plenitude of flush toilets, a rare enough item in Korea, where dwellers in hillside homes had to carry pails down to the valley to fetch water, and where little children ran about with holes in the seats of their pants, so they might deal with nature's demands, whenever and wherever the call came. The citizenry was further offended when Hodge went tooling about the city in a yards-long Cadillac with pearl fittings, the very car used by the Japanese royal family on their visits. Yet Hodge was not really a man to put on airs, and those Koreans who came to know him were usually attracted by his plain-spoken ways and outgoing manner.

Some biographers accused Hodge of saying out loud that Koreans were "the same breed of cat" as the Japanese. He said no such thing, for he had no such ideas. He was sym-

pathetic toward the Korean people and several times
directed his troops to treat them with respect, to be sure to
remove their shoes on entering Korean houses, to make no
advances to Korean women, to trade with the people fairly
and to honor their property rights. In fact, Hodge himself
went to such lengths to uphold the rights of the natives
that he was widely known, even among commissioned officers who might have been expected to own more sense
than the teen-age GIs, as a "gook lover."

The handicap of not having in his retinue anyone who
commanded even enough of the Korean language to bless
himself lay at the root of many of Hodge's difficulties. Neither State nor War Department had offered him any help
in this regard. Korea, in the minds of the folk in Washington (and in Tokyo) was the end of the line. When officers
were assigned to the Far Eastern Command, Tokyo
skimmed off the cream of the personnel and left the rest for
Hodge. Even the man put in charge of Korean affairs at the
State Department in Washington, Brigadier General John
Hilldring, knew little about Korea, probably less than
Hodge did. To Hilldring, Korea was an "occupied" rather
than a "liberated" country, and it took last place in his
concerns. But it took first place in Hodge's concerns, and
he protested strongly at his failure even to receive timely
information from State (or from Toyko) as to what was
being decided concerning his preserve. Even as late as February 1946, Hodge was still complaining to MacArthur
about the stepmotherly treatment he had received from
State. "I hope there is some way," his telegram said in part,
"in which you can pass on my ideas to the State Department and get over to them the thought that we must be
kept informed and that it might be worthwhile to consider
some of the information and recommendations we have

conscientiously sent in from the Korean hotspot based on fact and not on theory."

MacArthur himself had written off Korea before World War II ended. In a conversation with Brigadier General Paul Freeman, Jr., on June 13, 1945, MacArthur spoke of the need to bring Russia into the war against Japan. Freeman, who was not permitted to make notes at the interview but shortly afterward summed up what he had heard, reported that MacArthur "understands Russia's aims, that they would want all of Manchuria, Korea, and possibly part of North China. This seizure of territory was inevitable." It is a measure of MacArthur's sublime disregard for the truth that he blandly denied, during his abortive campaign for the Presidency, that he had ever recommended Russia's entry into the Pacific War.

Hodge thought that he had solved a good part of the problems of communicating with the Koreans when he chanced to overhear a U.S. Navy Lieutenant Commander talking to a Korean in the native tongue. He promptly appointed the naval officer as his "political advisor." Commander George Williams, son of a missionary family and a man of decidedly conservative, not to say reactionary views, probably could have set down all he knew about politics on the inside of a matchbook cover. But he did know a number of English-speaking and Christian Koreans, all of whom could have passed for right-wing Republicans in America, where some of them had received religious education. Many of them were landlords who had prospered under the Japanese and were about as popular among the plain citizens as the secret police.

It was the advice of these men that Hodge relied on in dealing with the People's Republic. He had kept Lyuh Woon-hyung out of his office for a month while he tried to

decide how best to cope with him and the "government" he
headed. His advisers confirmed Hodge's worst suspicions.
The People's Republic, they told him, was a rank Communist outfit and the People's Committees were mere mobs of
Communist gunmen. The People's Republic was indeed
strongly weighted with Communists, and its police force,
known as the "white-shirts" because of the white overgar-
ments they wore, kept order and collected "taxes" in standard Oriental style, with fist, gun and club. But the Committees were in many places volunteer organizations,
quickly formed to replace the vanishing Japanese, and included men of all shades of political opinion who were
working to keep some sort of government functioning.

When Lyuh's group, which had held a 600-delegate "national convention" in Seoul before Hodge's arrival, announced that it would conduct a national election to form a
legislature, Hodge, girded by his advisers' wisdom, directed
his military governor to issue a statement that read, in
part:

> There is only one government in Korea, south of 38 de-
> grees north latitude. It is the government created in accord-
> ance with the proclamations of General MacArthur, the Gen-
> eral Orders of Lieutenant General Hodge and the Civil
> Administration orders of the Military Governor. It is an orga-
> nization of carefully selected Koreans working under the
> Military Governor and his officers. It has exclusive control
> and authority *in every phase of government.* . . .
>
> A fraud on the people of Korea has been recently publi-
> cized in the free press, namely the calling of a fictitious elec-
> tion on the first of March 1946. . . . For any man or group to
> call an election as proposed is . . . an act of open opposition to
> Military Government and the lawful authority of the Gov-
> ernment of Korea under Military Government.

This hardly seemed the sort of statement a liberator would direct to the people he had set free, people who could not rid themselves of the notion that they owned the country and ought to have a voice in running it. The People's Republic responded with a pamphlet that recorded the pedigrees of the "carefully selected Koreans" who had been put in charge of government. One of them, Yu Uk Kyum, who was in charge of education, had actually recruited Koreans into the Japanese army during the war, and was among the most despised characters in the land.

The People's Republic remained defiant, even refusing an order to stop calling itself a government. (The word for "government" in Korea is *kook,* and this may have struck Hodge and his group as wryly symbolic. At the same meeting that the People's Republic refused to drop the word "government" they also voted to "cooperate fully with the American Command.") But Lyuh Woon-hyung, ambitious to lead a working government, and at the time the most likely choice of the people to do so, had already walked away from the "Republic" he helped to found and undertook to put together a new "People's Party" that would be free from Communist influence and thus more likely to suit the Americans. There were only five thousand Communist party members in Korea when the war ended, but they were well organized, with a specific program and an ideology to sell. Hodge, however, despite his apparent intent to deal evenhandedly with all sides, privately considered Lyuh a devout Communist who was simply putting on a disguise. In a report to the chief of the Civil Affairs Division of the War Department as late as January 8, 1948, six months after Lyuh had been killed, Hodge described Lyuh Woon-hyung as a "well indoctrinated Comintern Communist."

Hodge's conviction that it would be impossible to establish a democracy in Korea until the Communist influence had been eliminated reflected the feeling of MacArthur and of nearly all well-brought-up Army officers, who deemed all leftists, pinkos, Socialists and Communists as cats from the same litter. MacArthur, in a public statement, even included "dissenters," obviously never having discovered that dissenters were the very life blood of a democracy.

Raised as he was to believe in the magic of free enterprise, MacArthur approved a move by Hodge in September 1945 to feed South Korea a good dose of this elixir by removing all price regulations. The result was an explosion of inflation and speculation that soon saw most of the spring rice crop in the hands of speculators who sent the price rocketing out of sight. By summertime, there was actual starvation in South Korea, and almost half the people in Seoul had begun to mutter aloud that they were better off under the Japanese. Some southern farmers profited from hoarding their crops. But many poor folk quietly starved to death, while former collaborators gorged and speculators sold rice to distillers of liquor. When a Korean lady in Washington, Louise Yim, undertook at a later date to present a paper to the Secretary of War concerning starvation in South Korea, she was told it was "an insult to the War Department."

Hodge soon backed away from this experiment and reimposed rationing, with rice collections supervised by the military government. This looked to Korean farmers very much like life under the Japanese. In 1946, Koreans were granted, under the American Military Government, only about half what a Japanese was allowed. This, of course, merely deepened Korean discontent with Hodge's administration; even right-wingers began to complain that things were better when the Japanese were in control. Poor people responded with boycotts and riots. Some southern folk, repeating the misery of life under the Japanese absentee landlords, once more had to send their children out on the hillsides to pull up weeds and grass-roots for food. The situation was greatly worsened by floods that destroyed 20 percent of the crops. And the swelling of the population by the flood of refugees from the north cut the daily ration severely. The lack of sufficient American personnel to enforce the collection program was another aggravating factor.

The fear of "socialism"—reflecting, of course, the attitude of Tokyo and the qualms of powerful forces in the United States—also made it almost impossible for Hodge's government to work out ways of getting the former Japanese properties into Korean hands. The best that could be done, short of nationalizing the major enterprises, which MacArthur would never have permitted, was to hand them over to "managers," some of them American noncoms, who would run them for the benefit of the Property Custodian. Naturally, salaried managers quickly discovered ways of running such enterprises at least in part for their own benefit or for the benefit of those around them. Larger and larger quantities of goods began to trickle into the black market, and thousands of men and women who might have been discharged in the name of efficiency and greater profit under a free system were kept on payrolls.

As if these troubles were not sufficient to render Hodge's life almost insufferable (he told General Omar N. Bradley in a letter that he had "to walk several political tightropes at one time"), the political situation had degenerated, Hodge reported, "into chaos." It is doubtful that anyone alive

could have explained Korean politics to Hodge, for they
were almost an every-man-for-himself arrangement in
which any candidate who could hire a truck and a loud-
speaker might run for office or for leadership of some sort
on the same platform as several dozen rivals. (The workings of this system are lucidly explained in a fine book by
Gregory Henderson, *Korea: The Politics of the Vortex*.)

But Hodge, convinced that Communists were completely in the saddle in his zone, stuck to his resolve to rid
the land of this affliction. In this he had the strong backing
of MacArthur, who seems to have anticipated the Truman
Doctrine by developing his own plan for excluding the
Russians from the Japanese occupation and envisioning an
anti-Communist bastion in the Far East. Although Mac-
Arthur fathered, or at least sponsored, the creation of a
democratic constitution for Japan, ensuring freedom of
speech even for the far left, and had set Communists free
from the Japanese jails, he very quickly qualified these
freedoms when they proved embarrassing. After Japanese
prisoners of war, returning from Russian prison camps to
their homes throughout Japan, had been heard making
speeches about freedom and economic reform on railroad
station platforms, MacArthur's troops were ordered to silence them. And Hodge followed MacArthur's example
when the People's Republic took an open stand against
giving up their title as "government."

Steeped in the conventional wisdom that dissidents and
their like respond only to tough talk and firm action,
Hodge responded to the People's Republic in this manner:

> ... regardless of what it calls itself, the Korean People's Re-
> public is not in any sense a government ... The only func-
> tioning government in South Korea is the Military Govern-
> ment. .... in order to eliminate further misunderstanding and

cloaked disorders, I have today directed my occupation forces and the Military Government in Korea that the activities of any political organization in attempting operations as a government are to be treated as unlawful activities, and that necessary steps will be taken at once...

The People's Republic, in an angry rebuttal, pointed out that the Korean Provisional Government, newly arrived from Chungking with its president Kim Koo and all his "cabinet," after having assured the American command that they came as "private citizens," still used the word *kook* in its title, with no remonstrance from on high.

Hodge, however, moved ahead with the dismantling of the People's Republic, which was already functioning throughout Korea in some places where the Military Government had barely touched. In a few villages, it proved impossible to maintain any semblance of government at all without keeping the People's Committees in place. But eventually the People's Republic was eliminated, and with it went at least the first chance of transferring power in comparative peace to the Korean people.

Earlier, Hodge had considered his major problems solved when, born on official wings in the shape of MacArthur's personal plane, and apparently wearing the seal of approval from the State Department, there arrived in Seoul an old gentleman named Syngman Rhee (his name, given in Korean style, sounded more like Lyee Singmon), a Princeton-educated Ph.D. who was still a Korean patriot of renown with, everyone assumed, a devoted following among the plain people. MacArthur had taken him to his bosom only after Rhee's legitimacy as a confirmed anti-Communist and veteran Korean political leader had been vouched for by a committee set up for the purpose in Washington. Actually, the State Department had long since grown weary of the old man's importunities. He had been in Washington for some dozen years trying to promote the freedom and independence of his homeland— which no one in peacetime Washington gave a damn about. Rhee also sought support in Moscow, but turned violently anti-Soviet when the commissars closed their ears to his pleas. The committee that ultimately hallowed him was one put together by a former publisher of the *Brooklyn Eagle,* Colonel M. Preston Goodfellow of the War Department, who brought in, as representative of the Department of State a staunchly, not to say fanatically, anti-Communist lady whose job at State had been Chief of the Passport Division. Anointed by her hands, Rhee was provided with the papers he needed to reenter Korea (after thirty years) and flown off to meet MacArthur in Tokyo. To Hodge, who had been trying to fight his way through red tape to secure at least a knowledgeable adviser from State, Rhee must indeed have seemed heaven-sent. Here was exactly the popular leader needed to counterbalance those Reds in the People's Republic. Hodge provided him an escort, ration coupons, and a suite at Seoul's best hotel (eventually known to the American officer corps as the "Frozen Chosen").

There were policy makers in the Department of State who nearly went bananas when they learned that this old self-aggrandizer had been wafted off ostensibly to become leader of Free Korea. Immersed as they were in the job of trying to find ways of living in peace with the Russians, they suspected the aging doctor was carrying a political time bomb in his satchel. But channels between State Department and Tokyo were clogged with pride and protocol, and the course to Hodge was more difficult still.

Hodge himself soon had cause to wonder if there were

not a large helping of woe mixed in with this sudden blessing. He staged a welcoming meeting in Seoul for Rhee, and Koreans of every order gathered to cheer the old man's return. Without warning or invitation, Rhee promptly launched into an impassioned attack on Soviet Russia and Communism—a splendid tune indeed to most United States Army officers on hand but a series of very sour notes to most of the Koreans, who had not yet learned to think of Communism as an obscene word. Communists newly freed from years in jail for anti-Japanese activity were still hailed as heroes. And Hodge was more than mildly troubled himself. He had the present job of trying to work out with the Russians some way of uniting Korea under a native, democratically oriented government. But his troubles with Rhee had barely begun.

Soon after Rhee returned, the rest of the Provisional Government of Korea, led by its "president" Kim Koo, arrived, and then began the plots and maneuvers and counterplots that were to drive Hodge at last to the conclusion (expressed in his letter to General Omar N. Bradley) that the aim of every Korean politician was "personal and individual power, by fair means or foul."

Rhee, of course, envisioned himself as the eventual White Knight who would lead his land to freedom—even if he had to start with only half of it. Hodge had to stifle this ambition. And he had to cope with the angry and violent outbursts among the Korean citizenry that followed his dismantling of the People's Republic. He made frequent and sometimes frantic efforts to win from MacArthur or from Washington the help he needed to put together a coalition that would be neither reactionary nor Communist. But MacArthur, quick as he was to interfere in almost any situation that promised a bit of personal glory, had no taste for political hand-to-hand struggle. He had urged upon Hodge only that he protect the Koreans in their "personal and religious freedoms." He must have envisioned in Korea the sort of well-ordered society that decorated the copybooks of his youth, with well-fed and well-clothed youngsters bicycling down immaculate sidewalks, democracy asimmer on every hillside, and alabaster cities agleam in the valleys.

Kim Koo was no democrat any more than Rhee was, but he was ready to form a government with moderate leftists on board that might at least have given a rudder to the Korean ship of state, and permitted gradual transition to native rule. But Hodge would have none of this either. If Lyuh's group was not a *kook,* then neither was Kim Koo's, and MacArthur so far had shown no preference for anyone but Rhee. Kim Koo had been allowed to return only after he had solemnly promised to enter only as a private citizen.

As for officials at the Department of State, it took them three months to get around to telling Hodge that they wanted him to stay clear of Rhee. But Rhee had been strutting about with his Army escort all this while, making it clear that he was the chosen leader. And Kim Koo, who had been introduced to assembled correspondents under Military Government auspices, had reason to believe that his cause was favored. He had already made plans for a takeover on the first of the following March. Indeed, the State Department would have preferred to have him take over. But Hodge, with only his Army Manual to go by, canceled this election too and returned Korean politics to their normal state (at least since his arrival) of being all fouled up. He had been told many things not to do, but none of the mighty minds in Washington or Tokyo had given him any specific timely advice on how to accomplish his mission of building a democratic regime in Korea.

MacArthur, with characteristic indolence, had handed to Hodge the job of negotiating unity with the Russian command, a job Hodge was not equipped to handle, either by rank or by training. Now he had to take on that job without having yet created any sort of political unity in the section of Korea under his control. The Russians on the other hand, owning the advantage of coming to Korea with scores of Soviet-trained Koreans, who had served in either the Red Army or the Chinese Communist Eighth Route Army, had been able to slide their people right into control, working through the existing People's Committees. They continued to hide the Soviet face behind a native Korean front, and had won wide support (after some initial bitter hostility, owing to the rampaging of the Russian troops, who had fought the Japanese for two weeks or more after the surrender and had then run wild through the countryside) with a program of expropriation of Japanese property and extensive land reform. Land reform served the Russians too, for farmers who failed to support the new regime could have their land-ownership tickets taken away.

The most important immediate task facing Hodge was rebuilding the police force. Once the Japanese police had been dismissed and sent home, there were only a few thousand Koreans in the lowest ranks to keep order in the face of rising political violence and widespread crime. Even those Koreans who remained were, of course, Japanese-trained; it was on their account that Hodge made the breed-of-cat remark. (What he really said was that in the eyes of the Koreans themselves, the police who had been trained by the Japanese were the same breed of cat as the Japanese and they despised them just as heartily.) It was necessary, therefore, to try to find new recruits to replace most of the force.

Hodge was not quite able to manage this. He wound up by keeping most of the "cats" left behind by the Japanese and even signed up a few unsavory characters who had been chased out of North Korea by the Russians. With American officers to supervise them, the new Korean police turned out to be the one really cohesive political force in the nation. They were, naturally, sympathetic to the right wing, and to the extreme right wing at that. They were not at all hesitant at expressing their political leanings in action and systematically tempered their treatment of right-wing goons while visiting summary punishment frequently on the strong-arm men of the left. (Both sides in Korea used terrorism as a standard weapon.) General Hodge in reports to MacArthur apparently was unaware of this flagrant bias or simply condoned it, while MacArthur, of course, could not have been aroused by it either. At any rate, in a long critique of an unfavorable report by a Labor Department observer from the United States, Hodge staunchly defended the police. "They (the police)," Hodge wrote, "recognize Communist activities as subversive and tend to be a little rough on any subversive violence."

There was indeed plenty of violence to keep Hodge awake nights, but a more sophisticated officer, like Stilwell, would not have been so quick to belittle it all as pure Communist activity. When the populace in Taegu in October 1946 took up arms against the despised police, they did so as a result of very real abuses, and not merely because the local Communists told them to. The trouble began at a demonstration against the starvation diet, which the Koreans believed was caused by Military Government policies. In the rice collections the police consistently favored the right-wing citizens, who were, naturally, people of means. The South Korean Railroad Workers Association, seeking

better food and better wages, had called a strike throughout the land, and many strikers took part in the food protest. One policeman was badly injured in the course of the
Taegu demonstration and a striker was killed by police.

The next day a whole crowd of protesters carried the
striker's body to the steps of the police station and there
was immediate hell to pay. After a short battle, most of the
outnumbered police took to the hills and the mob ram-
paged through town, murdering policemen, mutilating
their bodies and dragging wounded police out of hospitals
to do them in. The rioting spread rapidly, and no Communists were needed to motivate it. Hatred of the police had
boiled in many Korean hearts throughout their lives.

Within a few days, there were antipolice riots in several
areas throughout the South, some of them heated up by
Communist agitators, who told of rice being taken up by
the Military Government and shipped to Japan, while Korean workers received second-rate grain. (There was
enough truth in this to make it convincing, for much
black-market food had gone to Japanese markets. Even
during the Korean war, one American officer in charge of
the docks refused to unload rice-laden Korean ships in
Japanese ports when there was hunger in Korea.)

The railroad strike itself turned into a major battle in
which right and left extremists fought each other with guns
and clubs. This too, in Hodge's eyes, was pure Communist
rebellion, and he afterward cited Communist literature to
prove it. (He did not explain why tens of thousands of
high-school students walked out in protest strikes.) The
fact that Russian- or North Korean-directed Communists
had an agenda different from that of the strikers, who
merely wanted money enough to live on, was no secret; nor
did it make the abuses the strikers complained against less

real. Hodge and his underlings were handicapped, not only
by their naïve Officers-club view that lumped all "leftists"
in the same noisome heap, but by their reliance on right-
wing interpreters to tell them the news. (The Military Government by this time was known as the "government of the
interpreters.") When Hodge summed up the strike story in
a report to the War Department, he gave a very distorted
picture indeed, insisting that the whole business was the
work of a Communist "minority" that, "through acts and
threats of physical violence," forced the workers to walk
out. A "show of force," he wrote, was necessary, to allow
the workers to return. As to Taegu, he noted that "sixty-
odd police were killed by Communist rioters." (Even
Major General Archer Lerch, Military Governor in 1947,
wrote to Hodge that in his opinion Communists did not
make up more than 10 percent of the Korean population
North and South.)

In his book, *Korea: The Politics of the Vortex,* Gregory
Henderson, who was one of the first Foreign Service officers to specialize in Korean affairs and who served over
seven years in the U.S. embassies in Pusan and Seoul,
gives a very different picture. While Hodge, in his report,
insisted that the strike began without warning or demands,
Henderson relates that, before the strike began, the South
Korean Railroad Workers Union submitted specific demands to the Military Government, including requests for
increased rice ration and pay allowance, and the end of
lay-offs, and the Military Government made no reply. The
strike spread then, according to Henderson, when a right-
wing union strong-armed its way in and police arrested two
thousand strikers. Riots followed throughout the nation.
While Hodge's investigations turned up not a single North
Korean agitator, police, before many months had passed,
had collected seven thousand political prisoners, some of

whom they treated to the methods made infamous under Japanese rule—kidney-punching, water-cure, electric
shock and the standard hanging by the thumbs. (Offensive
details of this nature did not appear in any of Hodge's reports to his superiors.) And MacArthur managed to add a
little gasoline to the fire by decreeing the death penalty for
any who raised their hands against the Military Government.

No doubt the Communists made much hay from these
matters, and no doubt many Koreans were won, at least
temporarily, to Communism. But Korea, like most agricul-
tural countries, was essentially conservative by nature, at
least in its desire to be left in peace, without any too-radi-
cal changes in its way of life. Still Hodge, like MacArthur,
clung to his conviction that Communism was an infectious
(and incurable) disease that had to be forcibly eradicated
before democracy could grow. The degree to which the
Military Government favored the right-wing, or any "anti-
Communist," grouping could be annotated endlessly.
"Leftists" found guilty (sometimes by hearsay evidence) of
acts of violence were sentenced to be hanged. A right-wing
killer of two was given seven years and another who tortured to death two leftist youths received a small fine.

In the aftermath of the Taegu antipolice riot, eighteen
ringleaders tried by the United States Army Military
Commission were sentenced to death. After appeal to
MacArthur, nine sentences were commuted to life impris-
onment and one man was set free. In rioting next spring,
there were over 2,500 arrests; "almost 100 percent of
these," General Lerch declared at a press conference,
"were leftists!"

Much violence of a different nature arose in Seoul as a
direct result of agitation by Syngman Rhee and his co-
horts, who received word of the decision of the Moscow

Conference that had decreed a five-year "protectorate" for
Korea. The Korean word for "protectorate" was the same
word used by the Japanese for their own rule and the immediate reaction of the Koreans who shared this news was
violent outrage. No one—neither State Department nor
MacArthur—had bothered to get early news of this matter
to Hodge, so Rhee's calling of a general strike took him
completely by surprise. And the walkout of Korean government workers, most of them loyal to Rhee, brought
Hodge's shop to a standstill. He and his staff made frantic
efforts to explain matters to the Koreans, assuring them
that the bad word did not mean quite what it said, and privately cursing the bureaucrats at home who had not at
least offered them time to think up excuses.

A number of Koreans had also enjoyed an advance look
at the result of the wartime conference in Cairo, where it
was decided that Korea should have her independence "in
due course." This document was smuggled into Korea before
the Japanese surrender, after the Provisional Government
in Chungking had translated "in due course" to mean "in a
short time." So, Koreans in Rhee's retinue at least had been
expecting not trusteeship but freedom, and that in far
less time than either the Americans or Russians had
planned.

There were other problems of equal concern to keep
Hodge awake at night in the first year of occupation. (At
about the time these troubles were gathering, he wrote to
Admiral Chester Nimitz that "this job is the worst I have
ever seen.") He was still intent on improving the relations
between American troops and the Korean people. He had
undertaken a "courtesy drive" early in the occupation
when he was disturbed by GI attitudes toward the native
population—the whistling at Korean girls, the practical

jokes on Korean males, high-speed driving through city streets, deliberate running of jeeps through muddy spots so as to splash and scatter waiting Koreans. He wrote to General Omar N. Bradley that he was displeased at the personnel coming his way, particularly the officers, and he told of troubles too with teen-age GIs.

This business of courtesy preoccupied Hodge for most of his stay in Korea. He was determined to impress on his troops that Korea was a liberated and not a conquered country. But there was always a bitter undercurrent of prejudice that he could not stem. And MacArthur's headquarters simply added to his woes by treating assignment to Korea as punishment. (One young soldier was offered his choice of court-martial or Korea.) The attitude of the unlettered and unregenerate GI was well exemplified in an interview by a *Chicago Tribune* reporter with a PFC from Oklahoma. "The worse that you treat Koreans," said the PFC, "the more he likes you. The only things they understand are the ball bat and the pick handle." And a PFC from Pennsylvania added: "The Koreans are hostile. You try to take a picture of a Korean child and he runs. You treat the Korean nice and he cheats you. You leave anything around, and the next minute it's gone." The captain of the company to which these young men belonged offered testimony that, in view of his rank, was equally dismaying—"The GI is wrong in some ways, but on the whole I am afraid he is justified in his attitude."

On a higher level, the Soviet-United States talks in Seoul to arrive at a method for unifying the nation under a democratically elected government had come to a dead stop on the question of voter eligibility. The United States delegation, headed by former military governor Archibald Arnold, had entered the discussions full of optimism, and full of ignorance about Korean politics. While MacArthur held himself aloof, Archer urged the South Koreans to form themselves into political parties in order to select spokesmen who might be consulted during the unification talks. He must have envisioned the sort of groupings he could have summoned up in America—Democrats, Republicans, Conservatives, Liberals, Socialists, and possibly a crackpot party or two with a private ax to grind. What he did not realize was that Korea had been so thoroughly bureaucratized under the tight control of the Japanese that there was no room for political parties. Indeed, the gathering of any groups with a common interest to influence the government in any way would have been deemed a conspiracy, subject to immediate suppression. Politics, to ambitious Koreans, had always been the road to individual advancement and the betterment of one's own fortunes, almost like getting ahead in business might have been for an American. One might resent, even intensely dislike the ownership, fret at the discipline, and grumble at the low pay, yet still feel loyalty to the company, be ready to follow orders and cater to one's superiors and look forward to a day when one's purse might be suddenly fattened enough to permit retirement to a life of ease.

At Arnold's call, it seemed that every man who could gather a few friends or neighboring farmers together under the same banner hastened to form a party and seek recognition. Arnold counted over four hundred political parties panting for acceptance, including one outfit that, pursuing God knows what common interest, called itself the "Full Moon Mating Society."

On their side of the fence, the Russians counted far fewer parties, and they had, of course, a well-organized and, on its face at least, native government to support their views. They practically shut the door on most South Koreans by insisting that no one who had failed to support the Moscow agreement on trusteeship could take part in the voting or in the consultations. That would have closed out everyone but the Communists and those they dominated. And the local Communists supported trusteeship only because they had been ordered to. Every self-respecting Korean hated the very sound of the word. The result of much haggling and compromising brought nothing more than an offer by the Soviets to grant suffrage to those who had not "actively opposed" trusteeship. And in practice this seemed to mean the same thing. Eventually General Archer had to give the whole thing up as a bad job, even after Secretary of State George Marshall had made an effort to win Molotov to a more relaxed stance. (Said Molotov: "As regards your reminder that no limitation of any kind of the freedom of word and opinion should obtain in the course of consultation, this must extend only to parties and organizations which cooperate in the realization of the Moscow Decision.")

Molotov also complained, with some justification, that the left-wing parties in the South had been subjected to searches, arrests and suppression, and that such a state of affairs was "inadmissible." But Hodge had made a sincere effort to hold Rhee's right-wing strong-arm men in check during consultations. When the deadlock was reached, he withdrew his protection and the police were turned loose on the leftists, with bloody results.

During the year, the Department of State finally sent a specific political directive to Hodge, urging him to form an interim government with "moderate" forces in charge. The moderates were to be led by one Kim Kiu-sic, with Lyuh Woon-hyung as vice-president. Kim, no relative of Kim

Koo, had been vice-president, under Kim Koo, of the Korean Provisional Government in Chungking. Hodge followed directions and soon had what appeared to be a functioning "Coalition Committee" of moderate hue, although he never did believe Lyuh was anything but a "Comintern Communist." Long careful "interpretation," supported by radio talks suggesting that trusteeship either was not going to be trusteeship at all or would be all over in no time, eventually won over the "moderates" to reluctant support of the Moscow agreement and provided some hope of reconvening the U.S.-U.S.S.R. Joint Commission. But the extreme right and the extreme left did their best to sabotage the operations of the moderates, and their first meetings were rocked by the railroad strikes and food riots that followed. Still, Hodge managed to hold the train on the tracks—probably a tribute to his own ability, in face-to-face contacts, to win the trust and support of Koreans. But he never became a fan of Lyuh Woon-hyung.

The Coalition Committee did last long enough to hold an election of sorts to create a Legislative Assembly in South Korea, with half of the delegates chosen by what passed for "popular" vote and half appointed by Hodge. The "election," which resulted in a sweep for the right-wing candidates, was a joke. In most villages, the headman cast all the votes at once, in the manner of an old-time Tammany boss; in other places, only landlords and taxpayers (i.e., the rich) could vote, as under the Japanese. Hodge redressed the balance somewhat by appointing candidates from the left of center. But no Communists. Indeed, Hodge bragged that all the members he appointed "hated Communism."

Even with the dilution of the strength of the extreme right wing, the "Interim" Assembly remained firmly reactionary. A number of the hairiest right-wingers walked out of the assembly in protest at the seating of the few leftists appointed by Hodge. They walked back again after having "saved face." And so, nothing was done to meet the most elementary demands of the peasantry—who still at that time made up over 80 percent of the population. They wanted land redistributed, just as MacArthur had divided up land in Japan, so tenant farmers might own the ground they worked. But the Assembly was weighted down with owners of great tracts of land, and they refused to vote to give it away, even though the Rhee contingent in that campaign had loudly pretended to favor land reform. So the Assembly did little to win the hearts of the plain people away from the enticements of the Communists, who preached land reform, the turning-over of Japanese assets to the people, and punishment of "collaborationists." (Inasmuch as it was impossible to make any headway in business, profession, or in laying up a competence under the Japanese unless you got along with the government, almost anyone who had prospered could be labeled a collaborationist.) As for Hodge and MacArthur, they were committed to wiping out all traces of Communism in South Korea. Regardless of the part he played in forcing the revision of the Japanese Constitution, MacArthur remained a McKinley Republican at heart, whose flesh crawled at the sound of "dissent." (He firmly opposed the income tax.)

Hodge's commitment to this cause led him in a dozen ways to strengthen and encourage the radical right, nor did he ever seem to learn that anti-Communism was never by itself cause enough to stir the blood of plain Koreans. As a matter of fact it is no cause even to arouse the fervor and fighting spirit of any considerable number of the exploited masses of the world, who are generally concerned with such matters as peace, land, and bread—words that often comprise the entire campaign program of Communist agitators.

The collapse into desuetude of the interim government was very nearly ordained by the turning-loose of the right-wing agitators and strong-arm squads, after the stalemate in the U.S.-U.S.S.R. Joint Commission. In the violence that followed, Lyuh Woon-hyung, still probably the most popular and most able of the non-Communist left and the favorite to head the government, was murdered on the streets on Seoul, within a few yards of a police box. Although some feeble efforts were made to lay this dark deed to Communist agents from the North, no one at or near the scene had any doubt that Rhee's killers had struck Lyuh down. With his death went the last faint hope that some sort of representative government might evolve which could deal on an equal basis with the North and perhaps achieve peaceful union.

The hope had been faint indeed, because Hodge could not throw a halter on Rhee, the anti-Communist with the most glamour and the most popular appeal. And Rhee was feeling his oats enough by this time to convince himself that he could even bump Hodge and Lerch, the military governor, right off the seat of power. He had been to Washington to plead his cause there and had left behind a tight little group, including Colonel Preston Goodfellow, who would carry the flag for him. When General Lerch himself went to Washington to try to coax out of an apathetic Congress enough money to keep Koreans from going hungry again, he ran head on into this group, and in private letters to General Hodge he explained what he was up against. In one of his first letters, dated July 14, 1947, Lerch told Hodge of allegations made by Rhee that Hodge was "trying to force Communism on the Korean people." The bitter irony of this charge must have put an extra crease or two in Hodge's brow.

But Rhee was apparently secure in the feeling that he had both the State Department and the War Department in his corner now. His "advisers" in Washington were telling him so and thus encouraging him in even more flagrant efforts to put Hodge and Lerch in wrong. Lerch did persuade most of the "advisers" to sign a radiogram warning Rhee of the danger that Congress would reject aid to Korea because of "common belief that Koreans are opposing Americans in Korea," and asking Rhee to wire that he was "behind American military authorities" in their efforts to aid Korea.

The reply from "Korpital" (Rhee's cable-code name for himself) contained no such assurance. Instead it alleged at considerable length, and with the use of Biblical parables, that Hodge had been "trying over a year to coax and coerce us to accept Trusteeship," even though Hodge had beseeched both Tokyo and Washington to drop trusteeship from the agenda. And it blamed the "appointee leftists" (named by Hodge) for passing "invalid" election laws—invalid because they contained "ridiculous clauses" to deprive pro-Japanese of voting rights. Rhee wound up his message by declaring that "we insist in carrying out in Korea President Truman's new policy regarding Communism and not General Hodge's own pro-Communist program."

In his letter commenting on this exchange, General Lerch, whose own program would have been for all foreign troops to pull out of Korea, because "from a military standpoint Korea is a liability to the United States," urged Hodge to invite Preston Goodfellow to visit Korea and give

Rhee the direct news that he was far off base. "Personally," Lerch wrote, "I think the old fellow has gone completely insane and I doubt very much whether it [Goodfellow's visit] would do any good, but I would certainly like to try before having to lock him up in jail."

Far from locking him up, they eventually were obliged, of course, to hail the self-seeking old man as the savior of his country and MacArthur's strong right hand in his battle against Communism.

MacArthur, meanwhile, seemed hardly to make note of these gathering woes that had almost overcome poor Hodge. Instead, SCAP, which was MacArthur's official acronym (Supreme Commander Allied Powers), was directing his intelligence officer, Major General C. A. Willoughby, to scold Hodge for, among other sins, sending a message to the Joint Chiefs of Staff about "Soviet inspired espionage in South Korea" before sending the same message to MacArthur, and for reporting "some arrests" of South Koreans without making clear that there had been a hundred. (A thousand would have been nearer the mark.)

But MacArthur and Hodge both rejoiced in the new Truman Doctrine for containment of Communism and bent with enthusiasm to putting it in force on their turf. Both men, of course, had *always* felt that the disease of Communism had to be subjected to quarantine, but Hodge had been handicapped by the decision of the State Department to put men like Lyuh into the government. While Hodge, good soldier that he had always been, tried hard to work a little left coloration into the government and MacArthur himself had been heard to say that the radical left was a necessity (sometimes) in Japan, neither man could put his heart into supporting a democracy so pure that it tolerated even "improper" dissent. MacArthur seemed, at least part of the time, to think of himself as a Southern aristocrat, even though his father had been a Union general of renown. (MacArthur received, every birthday, the biography of a Confederate general from his wife.) Hodge's political outlook, or lack of it, was clearly described in a letter he once wrote (but never mailed) to William Randolph Hearst, in January 1948.

The fight against Communism is an all-American fight here and elsewhere. As the U.S. Commander in Korea, I have been heartily engaged in that fight since September 8, 1945, not only fighting against Kremlin Communism and its propaganda supplied directly from the Soviet North Korean Occupation Forces, but handicapped by a lot of false and misleading information put out by the Communist, pinko and idealist liberal press of the United States. When we arrived here South Korea was in control of Kremlin Communists. . . . we have now eliminated danger of Communist control through educating the people to its dangers and cracking down on illegal activities. . . .

One must be allowed to conjecture that General Joseph Stilwell, had he been permitted to bring his Tenth Army to Korea in place of Hodge, would not have thought of his mission as the carrying on of a fight against Kremlin Communism. The Kremlin Communists, only weeks earlier, had been our staunch ally and ever-present aid. Even MacArthur, in typical MacArthur superlatives, had only recently hailed the Red Army for its glorious victories. From the date of the promulgation of the Truman Doctrine, however, MacArthur undertook to lead the crusade. Every officer who came to Korea, after briefing under MacArthur tutelage, arrived full of the determination to help build not exactly a free and independent nation, but a "bulwark against Communism." And, inasmuch as every-

one to one's own left looked like a Communist in that day,
it was necessary to move all the way over to Syngman
Rhee (Lerch always called him "Sigman" Rhee) to find a
position that was not vulnerable to political name-calling.

How difficult it must have been for Hodge to embrace
this old conniver may be gathered from other passages in
that same unmailed letter to Hearst. About his dealings
with Rhee, Hodge wrote in that letter:

> He has failed my hope for full success because of the fol-
> lowing basic faults:
> a. Intolerance and failure to reevaluate his people after 30
> years of absence . . . Anyone, regardless of ideology, who does
> not agree with his own ideas . . . is denounced as a Commu-
> nist or a traitor. His Austrian wife fans his ego. . . .
> b. Love for money and personal comfort. Since coming
> here he has tied himself up with . . . those Koreans who grew
> wealthy under the Japanese through full cooperation if not
> collaboration.
> c. Desire for personal power, which led him a year and a
> half ago to start a campaign for a separate South Korea that
> he could rule without regard for the entity of the nation.
> d. Development during the past year of what might be
> called a God complex, carrying with it the fixed idea that he
> and he alone should dictate to his people without advice
> from anyone. . . .
> Many of his attacks [on me] have followed the best Com-
> munist vein—so much so that many well-informed Ameri-
> cans here are prone to believe that he has sold out to the
> Russians.

There is something poetic indeed about Rhee's and
Hodge's calling each other Communist. But that was a
standard tactic in the Cold War era, when some hint of the

Communist taint could be found in just about everyone, what with the Communists having shifted their own targets in so swift and bewildering a fashion. (Nearly everyone alive at that time could vividly recall when Communists, on order, had been toasting the sincere and lasting friendship between Soviet Russia and Nazi Germany.)

Of course, as the Cold War intensified, it would have taken far more magic than lay in the hands of Hodge and MacArthur and all their men to put North and South Korea together again. But steps taken by both men, sometimes unthinkingly, continued to aggravate the violence between extremists of both right and left. The Military Government's bias toward the right, or toward what American officers generally thought of as "the better people," was almost automatic. Most of them had been raised as Teddy Roosevelt had been, in the faith that well-educated, well-nurtured, neatly groomed, and properly dressed folk had been created by God to govern the rest of us. One man in South Korea, to his utter amazement, was named mayor of his village by the Military Government because he was the only one in the crowd who had a necktie on.

When the Military Government undertook to set up a "youth group" that would raise up young people in the way they should go, hardly anyone in the military concerned himself with the fact that the sponsors of the movement in each community were the property owners and leaders in business, people who, as William Langdon, political adviser to the Military Government put it in a report to the State Department, "inevitably favor the rightist parties [and] will choose youths whom they consider possessed of 'proper ideas.'"

And when American correspondents made so bold as to find fault with the degree to which the Military Govern-

ment favored the extreme right wing, Hodge did not hesitate to suggest that they too might be secret Communists.
Gerald Walker of the *Christian Science Monitor* wrote a
long story for his paper which contained the assertion that
"they [most observers] would mention policies which, deliberately or not, resulted in Korean rightists receiving
preferential treatment over leftist groups ..." Hodge
promptly wrote to MacArthur, who had inquired about
this "penetrating Communist," and declared "I consider
this typical Communist distortion ..." even though State
Department advisers and others who could be judged at
least reasonably impartial had made the same charge.
Hodge also bristled at the fact that Walker, in reporting a
hearing on the police situation, spoke of "a clear and con-
cise picture" given by one critic of the police and of "even
clearer testimony" given by another, but did not use any
adjectives at all to describe the testimony of the Director
of the Police.

Said Hodge in his letter to SCAP: "The general picture
of the activities and attitude of Walker ... is indicative of
the action of one within the Communist circle who is
working under the guise of a representative of a reputable
publication ..."

Hodge also wrote to Erwin Canham, editor of the *Christian Science Monitor,* quoting what he called "fairly reli-
able" sources to the effect that Walker was "very hostile to
the American effort to prevent Communism from taking
over."

A short time later, Hodge withdrew his objections to
Walker, who, he said, "showed a desire to report news ob-
jectively."

Other "Communists" showed up in more sensitive quarters from time to time and Hodge tried to have them

rooted out. The publication *Stars and Stripes* underwent a
purge to get rid of editors who kept referring to officers as
"brass" and Major General Orlando Ward reported to
Hodge that he was looking into "possible Communist
background" of soldiers who had griped about poor dental
care, lack of light bulbs, lack of showers, lack of brooms,
and waiting months for eye care. These "11 sissies"
(Ward's phrase) had written to Cecil Brown of the Mutual
Broadcasting System, and Brown had aired the com-
plaints. It is true, Ward admitted, that the dental situation
is bad and the eyeglass situation not too good and we are
"still very short on brooms" and there is trouble about
water for showers in some places, but "light bulbs are improving." (During our Civil War in the previous century a
Union soldier complained that the only whiskey they ever
got from the commissary was made up of "bark juice, tar-
water, turpentine, brown sugar, lamp-oil, and alcohol."
Nobody called him a Communist.)

Hodge's intense suspicion of all leftist opinion led him to
ignore sound advice from impartial and well-intentioned
folk who put in long hours investigating the Korean situation and articulating their ideas. Roger Baldwin, head of
the American Civil Liberties Union, submitted a thoughtful report to Hodge that seems to have received no more
than passing notice. The ACLU was, of course, an outright
Communist outfit in the eyes of MacArthur and his court.
Baldwin's report to Hodge included the following suggestions:

> ... the United States ... can be persuasive through pub-
> licity in getting laws adopted. One of the first should be a *bill
> of rights* to establish a democratic basis.... prosecutions
> under American ordinances out of line with the Bill of Rights

should be stopped . . . Criticism of the U.S. occupation policies in a liberated country should be permitted where it does
not impinge on military security—a fine line to draw. . . .

It would be futile from a democratic point of view to hold
an election before some sort of purge is undertaken, at least
of the top collaborators, and before the peasant demand for
land distribution is satisfied. . . .

The problem of securing a responsible and non-political
police force should be more effectively handled by placing
the police under the civil government and a commission,
with directions from the Military Government to clean up
lawless, corrupt, and collaborationist elements.

The censorship of all mail, foreign and domestic, would
appear to be unnecessary in a liberated country and should
be abandoned. Any really subversive material is not sent by
mail.

Experience shows that the best way to meet the threat of
Communist domination is by a vigorous and successful democratic policy. Anti-Communism is in itself no answer. . . .

While these suggestions hardly read like excerpts from
Joe Stalin's catechism, Hodge and MacArthur apparently
viewed them as mere facets of the Comintern line. For
when Hodge sent on to MacArthur a lengthy critique he
had written on a report by Stewart Meacham of the Labor
Department, who had come to Korea to act as Labor Advisor to the Military Government, Hodge advised Mac-
Arthur not to bother reading the Meacham report. "It follows," he wrote, "the Roger Baldwin–Mark Gayn–Hugh
Deane line." And anything that followed a line in those
days was *ipso facto* a Communist device.

It was in following the new Truman line, of course, that
the Military Government had to shake hands with the
devil by giving its blessing to Syngman Rhee. For not just

in Korea, but all over the globe, we began to create bulwarks out of the creaking timbers of reactionary, even corrupt, regimes, on the theory, expressed in so many words
one day by C. D. Jackson of the Time Inc. publications,
that we could not afford to build democracies because we
"have a pistol at our heads."

Of course, given the determination of the Soviets to create at all costs a friendly, not to say submissive, regime at
their back door and to undermine any bulwarks that might
be abuilding there, it would by this time have taken political genius and patience of a much higher order than had
ever been granted to MacArthur and Hodge to avoid a
head-on confrontation.

But MacArthur seemed determined to lend Hodge no
hand at all in trying to find the elusive middle way between
Rhee and the moderate left. The extreme left, unlike the
extreme right, being totally excluded, even banished, from
the scene, the "middle" was bound to lie some distance to
the right of center, so Hodge's mission was almost mathe-
matically impossible anyway. But he was trying dutifully,
and in spite of his own prejudices and inability to commu-
nicate, except through interpreters, to find some combina-
tion of forces that did not wear the face of reaction and ab-
sentee-landlordism. Had he not habitually classed all
"leftists" as enemies of the common weal as well as of the
Military Government, his task might have been less complicated. And had he had someone upstairs less grandiose,
less indolent, and possessed of more sidewalk savvy than
MacArthur, he might not have had the job wished on him
in the first place.

As it was, South Korea went into the U.N.-supervised
election—which was intended to be held nationwide, except that the Russians would not permit the U.N. officials

to cross the 38th parallel—with Syngman Rhee the only
figure around whom the Koreans could unite. And Rhee
had more than once sounded his determination to unify
Korea by force. While the election undoubtedly, from lack
of observers enough to cover more than a tiny fraction of
the polls (thirty U.N. observers for the whole southern half
of the nation), was tilted artificially toward the right, it did
reveal how tenuous was the hold these supposedly ubiqui-
tous and fearsome Communists held on the plain people.
For the people participated wholesale, turning out in every
corner of the land as on a national holiday to mark ballots
and drop them in the boxes, even though the organized
Communists employed every means, including violence, to
keep citizens from voting for any candidate at all. Surely
some less hidebound and more daringly democratic effort
might have managed to take advantage of this almost uni-
versal enthusiasm for taking part in designing their own
new government without Communist direction. As it was,
with a legislature practically owned, or at least terrorized,
by Syngman Rhee, the last hope of peace between North
and South had expired.

This very result had been foreseen by Dr. Arthur Bunce,
State Department economic adviser to the Military Government, who had spent six years in Korea. In January
1947, Dr. Bunce had written to George Atcheson, his immediate superior in Tokyo, to summarize "the position in
Korea." He wrote:

> It appears essential that the present liberal policy of Gen-
> eral Hodge should be strongly supported in Washington . . .
> The extreme rightists, associated with elements of the Dem-
> ocratic Party, Dr. Rhee and Mr. Kim Koo, have built up a
> political machine that is very powerful; they have also great

popular appeal on the basis of the stand they have taken against trusteeship. At the same time this group has the support of all the wealthy Koreans who are accused of "collaboration" with the Japanese, the landlords, and those who held office under the Japanese. The group has opposed the free land distribution program and the Moscow decision on Korea. It is my firm conviction that to give political power to this group would lay the foundation of ultimate civil war in Korea; meanwhile it would make any settlement between the U.S. and the U.S.S.R. regarding the unification of the country difficult or impossible.

For these reasons I believe that the middle of the road policy now being followed is the only one that is sound from the point of view of our interests and those of the Korean people. To follow this policy will not be easy, nor is there any guarantee that it will be successful. The alternative of giving power to the extreme right, however, is so fraught with danger that it can hardly be considered a valid alternative.

In my discussions with various members of General MacArthur's staff regarding the possibility of the Commanding General visiting Korea to use his prestige and influence to support this policy, I received a very negative impression. . . .

I am not certain that General Hodge can or will follow the present "middle of the road" policy without outside support. At the same time I believe that to relinquish this policy will result in serious repercussions. . . ."

There can be no doubt that a "negative impression" from the MacArthur court was a flat "No!" from his Imperial Highness. There was no hay to be made for MacArthur in trying to steer the wobbly Korean machine over that rough way toward unification and democracy.

2

---

minor matters

In speaking, not long ago, of the visit of a Foreign Service inspector to Tokyo when MacArthur was serving as Supreme Commander there, John Muccio, former United States Ambassador to the Republic of Korea, related that the hapless inspector had never been able even to poke his nose inside the United States Embassy, where MacArthur and his family were in residence. "MacArthur," said Muccio, "ran him out of Tokyo." Indeed he ran him right out of Japan, because, during MacArthur's reign, no outsider could stay in that land without MacArthur's authorization.

Yet MacArthur was not ordinarily an antisocial person. While to many he might have seemed arrogant and aloof, he was, in face-to-face meetings, friendly, considerate, good-humored, sometimes fatherly, even affectionate, fond of banter, and possessed of great personal charm. And though he never permitted undue familiarity in subordinates, or even those of equal rank, he would frequently disarm an uneasy colleague by dropping a hand on the

man's shoulder, or offering a friendly pat. Still, he had few
real intimates. Almost none of his peers, once he had attained high rank, ever called him "Douglas" except his
mother and Franklin Roosevelt. He signed his letters to his
wife "MacArthur" and she addressed him as "Dear Sir
Boss"—a title borrowed from *A Connecticut Yankee*.
(Said one colleague who knew them both: "She was scared
to death of him." But that might be said of many devoted
wives.)

Still, the inspector, like everyone else who attempted to
peek behind the façade to find what went on in Mac-
Arthur's private life had the door firmly closed in his face.
The day after the MacArthurs left Tokyo, however, one
lady who inspected the embassy reported it was a "sham-
bles," windows denuded of drapes, carpets worn bare,
stuffing bursting out of the upholstery. And servants, she
exclaimed, "coming out of the walls!"

Such matters, of course, would be of less moment than
the weather in Waco, Texas, on some forgotten Sunday,
except that they apparently symbolize MacArthur's lifelong concern for the external image and his disregard of
"detail." When Vice-Admiral James Doyle, charged with
staging the Inchon landing, sought an interview with the
big chief a few days before the landing was scheduled, to
apprise him of some obstacles that needed reckoning with,
he was refused admittance. "The General," MacArthur's
Chief of Staff told him, "is not interested in minor matters." Fortunately for the nation, and for the men whose
lives were at stake, Admiral Doyle was not to be diverted
by the likes of General Edward M. Almond, and he kept his
foot in the door until he was finally admitted. He succeeded, for one thing, in winning agreement on some preparatory bombardment to precede the actual landing. Mac-

Arthur had been all for total surprise. Doyle felt it would be suicidal to put forces ashore without previously cutting down on the enemy firepower. Surprise, by that time anyway, would have been partly an illusion, for the news of the landing had been picked up by dozens of the countless spies who infested the Japanese waterfronts, and had been spread clear to Korea.

MacArthur, throughout his career, had exhibited special skill at closing his eyes to details. Dr. D. Clayton James, in *The Years of MacArthur,* tells of MacArthur's plan to stage a great parade in Manila with the Philippine forces of which he had been named Field Marshal (a title he had selected for himself, even designing the lushly braided cap to go with the title). When his aides Colonels James B. Ord and Dwight D. Eisenhower tried to enlighten him about the extreme difficulties that lay in the way of gathering all these forces from throughout the archipelago, MacArthur simply bade them be silent. But when the Philippine president exploded at the notion, declaring that he had neither the funds nor the transport for any such show, MacArthur turned on his aides, blamed them for suggesting the grand parade, and publicly chewed them out for ever promoting such folly. Eisenhower and Ord were left openmouthed.

Dr. James also describes the complete state of unreadiness of these troops when the Japanese attack finally came. MacArthur had officially predicted it could not come before 1942 and ridiculed the War Department's War Plan Orange as "defeatist." That plan had called for phased withdrawal to the Bataan peninsula, where preparations were to be made for a protracted siege, until relief could be sent from the United States. Gulled by MacArthur's persuasiveness and by his self-proclaimed expertise in all matters Oriental, the War Department had agreed to depend for defense on MacArthur's forces, which were to keep watch on all the beaches, meet the enemy wherever he tried to land, and then drive him back into the sea.

When the Japanese forces did land, however, the Philippine army collapsed. They had neither steel helmets nor entrenching tools. Many did not own a blanket or even a coat. They had no modern rifles, and some did not carry any firearms at all. In each of the three divisions of this "army" there were two or three regiments that had received no training whatever. Many had not even fired their rifles on the range. Their commander, General Jonathan Wainwright, quoted by Dr. James, said, "Few of my forces had been completely mobilized and all lacked training and equipment." Many of them, indeed, fled into the hills at the moment of attack and never came back again.

Other "details" that escaped MacArthur's attention were the cleaning up of the Bataan peninsula, preparatory to its defense; the stockpiling of food and medical supplies; and the building of fortifications. As a result, the American troops who set up their final defense there were soon wracked by malaria, and went on half rations almost from the very day they settled in. Food at Corregidor was far more plentiful and no one starved.

MacArthur, who had an understanding with President Manuel Quezon that he would resume his highly paid job as Field Marshal as soon as the unpleasantness was over, had counted on a strong guerrilla movement to prevent the Japanese from ever getting a tight hold on the Philippines. He apparently gave no thought whatever to feeding the American troops, who would ultimately provide the only organized defense. Warehouses full of rice were left unmolested while empty army trucks rolled on to Bataan. Had the peninsula been at least partly treated with pesticide, had there been medicine enough to cope with the crippling diseases, had there been food enough to keep the men healthy and alert, had there been armament and fortifications of sufficient strength to provide steady resistance, the doomed peninsula might well have held out two or three times longer than it did—possibly even long enough to have received help from home.

MacArthur, however, had on his mind other matters than details of defense. It has even been suggested that he expected the Philippines to remain neutral in the war and thus be exempt from Japanese bombing. He certainly made no effort to save his air force—mostly parked wing to wing on Clark Field when the Japanese bombers came calling—although his apologists and courtiers all hastened to lay the blame on General Lewis H. Brereton, in command of the air force there, for not having his planes in the air as soon as the news of Pearl Harbor had been broadcast. But General Brereton had sought in vain to reach MacArthur to get authority for sending his planes on a bombing raid against Japanese strongholds. He was not allowed past the door.

MacArthur's distaste for detail persisted throughout his term in Tokyo. When the first occupation troops landed, many of them already battle-weary, the common soldiers often found no decent housing awaiting them and some of them did not even find food. Sergeant Frederic Donner of the 307th Infantry Regiment has a letter on file in the archives of the United States Army Military History Institute wherein he describes conditions under which he and his mates were traveling when they were being carried on a Japanese destroyer from one port to another, just after the war had ended.

> . . . I found a room [Donner writes] with shelf bunks covered with straw mats. One light bulb in room. I stacked my gear in the corner, used my pack and helmet to lie on the mats and

lay on the edge so I could get out as dozens of soldiers were crowding into the room and crawled over me into the shelf bunk. I felt things dropping on my face and hands. I looked up at the ceiling and saw hundreds of cockroaches. I raised the short mats and under them were hundreds more. That was enough. I got up and went on deck. . . . The toilet was a wood outhouse built on the deck and rail. The outlet was a trough running the length of the deck, with holes occasionally for excess to run out. The stench was horrible . . . As the ship pitched and rolled it sloshed back and forth and ran around the deck.

Donner also described life in the first replacement depot outside Yokohama:

I was in a casual company and we had to clean out the flea-ridden straw on floors of Jap barracks which had no windows with glass, only open buildings. We had no lights except candles some troops had and it was cold nites and the damp penetrated to the bone, and rains kept the area around the building all mud . . . Food was almost non-existent for more than a week. An occasional truck would go thru the area and K rations thrown off to be caught or picked up by troopers. It was a big mess. Buildings with windows which could be heated were designated for officers' files and desks. Other windowed buildings were assigned to officers as quarters, mess hall and bakery. Cake was baked for officers' mess, along with bread, while the troops were on rations.

The workings of the brutal army caste system under MacArthur's reign had other aspects that Donner did not fail to make note of. When he was assigned to duty at the laundry, he had a superior officer who required to be awakened every morning at ten. Donner described the scene in the bedroom when he went to shake the man awake. The room was always "foul smelling" and there would be "Jap

naked girls laying around," while the officer himself would
be sprawled dead asleep on his cot, "many times with
vomit all over his shirt." Donner would have to call in two
Japanese workers from the laundry to clean the officer up
and straighten up the room. Donner, at another point, described an officer of the airborne troops who appeared on
the road wearing a tam o'shanter on his head, leading a
French poodle on a leash and carrying a swagger stick
under his arm. This was at Camp Kreis in Sapporo, where
Donner and his mates pulled guard duty, two hours on and
two off, in driving snow and thirty-below-zero cold, until
snow was piled deep on shoulders and rifle and clung to his
pants. His nose froze, his eyes were rimmed with ice and
his breath froze his woolen mask to his whiskers.

It might be worth noting that during this occupation period, Lieutenant Alexander Haig, then on the staff of General Almond, MacArthur's Chief of Staff, was asked to send
a letter to the Brandt Cabinet Company in Hagerstown,
Maryland, on Mrs. Almond's behalf, asking them to send a
book they offered entitled *Table Tips for Lovely Living*.

Eventually, when the combat troops had been largely
repatriated and replacement had begun to flow into Mac-
Arthur's realm from the States, life for the lower ranks
started to improve—but not in the direction of spit and
polish or a more zealous *esprit de corps*. Youngsters were
urged to enlist for occupation duty in order to savor the
delights of the Orient. And these were largely delights of
the flesh. Combat training became almost an afterthought.
Narrow Japanese roads offered too little room for tank
training. Hillsides were closely cultivated and would have
been chewed up unduly by maneuvers. Besides, it had become an item of faith that the next war, if there were to be
one, would be fought with nuclear arms entirely, and that

civilians would do most of the dying. The government at home, rejoicing in the end of rationing and the sudden surge of peacetime spending, threw away its arms as if they never wanted to see or hear of them again. Planes that might have effectively bolstered the ground forces in Korea and armament that could have been moved quickly to increase the firepower of the first troops engaged in Korea had all been abandoned or buried or sold in Europe and in Okinawa.

Still, it was MacArthur's assignment to see to the defense of Japan. He devoted about as much attention to this as he had to the defense of the Philippines. And his own indolence was clearly reflected in the attitude of the occupation troops toward their assignments. They never learned how to act in battle. They learned nothing about night fighting or about fighting in mountainous terrain like that in Korea and Japan. Instead, they were employed, (according to reports in *Time* magazine) in "putting down Communist agitators, collecting taxes, and chasing smugglers." Many of them, if they had no soft noncombat-type jobs in the Army, sought civilian jobs that helped fatten their incomes and widen their ranges among the bars and beer parlors, where friendly companions and complaisant ladies were always in good supply. One American general, irritated by the "garrison" attitude, made a point of asking sharp questions of any GI he found wandering about unsunburned. Even sergeants on occupation duty employed "batmen" to take over all the unpleasant chores and run the errands. (When General Matthew B. Ridgway assumed command of the Eighth Army in Korea he aroused resentment among some of the sergeants by ordering them to get rid of their man-servants.)

The officer corps, quite naturally, took to the sybaritic

life even more avidly than the enlisted men did. Catered cocktail parties, where the grimmest duty was getting regally drunk, were standard operating practice whenever a new officer flew in or an old one said his farewells. General F. W. Moorman, who arrived in Tokyo near Christmas time in 1950, to join General Ridgway in Korea, found to his dismay that he was an object of pity at Tokyo headquarters among the officers, who provided him a lavish welcome. "Korea?" they asked him. "God, that's too bad! Can't you get out of it?" (Moorman, like most seasoned officers, had counted it a privilege to be assigned to the spot where the action was hottest.)

The troops assigned to Korea, before the American forces were withdrawn, were doubly embittered by the contrast between their lot and that of the men who remained behind in Tokyo. For them no glasses tinkled and no willing girls sang. They ate C rations while their officers bitched about the lack of ice cream. Some had to seek sleep and recreation in squalid huts without lights, far from transportation and often without proper clothing. They were, you may be sure, the last people in the mind of MacArthur, whose eyes sought far horizons and triumphs yet unsavored. In royal seclusion, he played the part of the Emperor, whose being he had supplanted in the daily life of the Japanese.

Austere, aloof, autocratic in all his public appearances, yet peaceful in his demeanor, with none of the vindictiveness the Japanese looked for in a conqueror, MacArthur won worshipful admiration from most of the Japanese, at least until it became clear that the Americans were not going to allow the labor unions to push their cause *too* far, at which point there began to grow, on the left, a bitter opposition to the occupation.

MacArthur had first won the respect of the Japanese by appearing without arms or any show of arms when his airplane landed. (In Korea, MacArthur ordered all the officers to wear side arms, as in a conquered country.) And he remained a mystic and superhuman figure.

Unlike Matthew Ridgway, who succeeded him, MacArthur never mixed with the common people of Japan, never visited a Japanese home, seldom traveled far off his daily route between his home at the former American Embassy and the Dai Ichi (Number One) Insurance building, where he maintained his headquarters.

MacArthur's "work" day began about ten-thirty in the forenoon, included a long break at two o'clock for lunch and a nap, and then continued from five-thirty until nearly midnight, with no regard for the fact that his staff, who had come to work at eight or nine, might have to stay on duty thirteen or fourteen hours just to be on hand if he wanted them.

MacArthur almost never held staff meetings, allowed no telephone in his office, kept no papers on his desk, and often busied himself by reading over even the most trivial messages that might be coming and going through his headquarters. He handled his own publicity, but he often allowed his letters to be written by his alter ego, Major General Courtney Whitney, a Manila lawyer and mining promoter who had helped MacArthur get rich in gold-mine speculations.

Whitney, one of the most despised men in Tokyo, or in the entire army for that matter, has been described by one MacArthur colleague as "a blue-water son-of-a-bitch." He was, like so many of MacArthur's pets, an arrogant man with a caustic tongue and an overbearing manner, a practicing anti-Semite, and an ardent self-seeker. But he aped his idol so closely that MacArthur once allowed that even he could not always tell which letters he had written himself and which had been written by Whitney. It seems almost certain that Whitney must have written the *Reminiscences,* for they contain some misstatements so obvious that one cannot conceive of MacArthur's having committed them to paper, quick as he surely was to warp facts to his own advantage.

In the *Reminiscences,* for instance, as General Ridgway pointed out in his own book about the Korean war, MacArthur "remembers" the defeated and disheartened South Korean army retreating in clouds of dust, although it had actually been raining for days. Whitney was not at the scene, but General Almond, MacArthur's Chief of Staff, was. And General Almond's description is almost the opposite of MacArthur's (or Whitney's), not only as to the weather but concerning the appearance, armament and bearing of the troops. Although the *Reminiscences* tell about South Korean troops that were "panting" and "disorganized," whose "weaving lines" were "interspersed here and there with the bright red crosses of ambulances filled with broken, groaning men," there was no such picture in MacArthur's words to Almond after the visit to the front:

"I've seen many retreating Korean soldiers during this trip, all with guns and ammunition at their side, and all smiling and I've not seen a single wounded man. Nobody is fighting."

General George Marshall once said that when an army's morale is lacking, the commander should look to his own. And the army of occupation in Japan, and particularly many of its officers, seemed to reflect much of MacArthur's own failure to take any thought for "detail." Of course, the army suffered too from the peace fever at home that had

cut military manpower and allowed weapon supply to
peter out. When war came in Korea, the troops in Japan
were short of noncommissioned officers, short of weapons,
and generally understrength. To meet the manpower
shortages imposed by the lowered 1948 draft, the I and IX
Corps had been eliminated from the Eighth Army, and the
infantry regiments had been reduced from three battalions
to two, while artillery regiments as well were cut from
three batteries to two. Occupational-type and service units
were also eliminated, so that, according to General John
Michaelis, it was impossible to activate the desired combat
support and service units when they were needed.

Combat-effectiveness training had been instituted about
nine months before the Korean fighting began, with squad,
platoon and company exercises conducted under regimental supervision. The "problem" was a Russian invasion of
Hokkaido. But the colonels who commanded the regiments were too often men who had had no wartime command experience. Instead they had been leading the life of
retired country squires, with handsome quarters, private
gardens, oversize household staffs, chauffeured staff cars,
and all the perquisites of "lovely living." And they were, in
the words of General Michaelis, simply "not qualified
physically or professionally to carry on when the rigors of
combat were imposed on them."

The trouble was that, when new officers were assigned to
the theater, MacArthur headquarters simply cannibalized
the best of them. On arrival, all were held in Yokohama,
while their personnel records were assessed. Those who
stood highest were selected by GHQ and what was left
went to Eighth Army, where they were promptly labeled,
privately and sourly, "Reject Number One," "Reject Number Two," and so on.

The fresh troops too were assigned on a priority basis, with the 1st Cavalry at the top of the line and the 7th Infantry at the bottom. But when the alarm sounded, and despite their nine months' training at the Mount Fuji maneuver area, they nearly all found themselves completely unprepared for combat. No one had told them *they* might have to fight. It simply wasn't fair! Physically, mentally, emotionally, they were geared for peace and plenty.

General (then Lieutenant-Colonel) Michaelis was one regimental commander who had had extensive combat experience. Before reaching Yokohama he had already accepted an invitation from General Walton Walker, commanding the Eighth Army, to join Walker's G-3 (operations) Division as deputy. When the call came to land troops in Korea, Michaelis was named commanding officer of the 27th (Wolfhound) Regiment of the 25th Division, and he first met his troops at Pusan in early July. They were among the first to land in Korea. And they were scared! Some of them, according to Michaelis, were even afraid to be out in the dark. And many of their officers were themselves seeing spooky things at their shoulders.

They had completed basic training satisfactorily. But they lacked proper training, at the small-unit level, in scouting and patrolling, reduction of stoppages and such matters. At battalion and regimental level they had not been trained properly in the combined use of their own crew-served weapons and the supporting artillery. And the brave young pilots were entirely useless in close air support—they could not even recognize ground targets.

In one of his publicity releases soon after fighting began, MacArthur spoke of the "excellent peacetime training" that had provided the ability with which these troops were fighting "one of the most skillful and heroic holding actions in history." This may have been forgivable wartime exaggeration, but heroic as the action was—and there were many wholly unsung feats of gallantry to balance the outright panic that seized some—there were still hundreds of soldiers involved who simply did not know what to do when the enemy was upon them. And all were brutally handicapped by a terrifying lack of proper weaponry. The 2.36 rocket launcher with which the Americans were equipped was wholly ineffective against the Russian-made tanks; it would not penetrate the armor. The 105-mm. antitank shells with which the artillery had been provided were quickly used up. According to men at the scene, the North Korean tank columns simply swept the first American troops aside without slowing down. There was also a desperate shortage of 4.2 mortar ammunition.

C rations too—the only ration that would provide a reasonably balanced meal—were in short supply, so that the small units necessary to hold the high ground along the main supply route received only B rations, and those only twice a day, and hardly ever in balanced fashion. Some units, for instance, might receive all beans, another all beef, another beets and beans, another nothing but beets. To supply them with water and ammunition was a nightmare. No cold springs flowed on the barren ridges, and drinking water had to be toted up from the valleys. Heat and germ-laden dust bore down on everyone. Fatigue and diarrhea added to the general distress. Still, the troops, in the school of bitter combat, learned fast how to stay alive and how to inflict damage on the enemy.

When Colonel Michaelis' troops took up their first defensive position—at Antung—Michaelis had a map supplied by the regimental S-2 (intelligence) that bore red arrows pointed at their position from three directions, each

carrying the annotation "5–10,000 NKs." At Army headquarters at Taegu, Michaelis recalls, there was the same
tendency to see thousands of bad guys behind every rock.

What later incensed some of the participants was to read
MacArthur's boast that he had thrown his troops "piecemeal" into the conflict as part of his own well-thought-out
plan to "fool" the enemy commander into thinking the
American forces were far stronger than they really were. A
great many historians accepted this appraisal of the manner in which the troops were committed to the fight and
have also characterized this move as "brilliant." But some
of those in a position to judge, including at least one Pentagon officer who was in constant touch with the situation,
characterized MacArthur's statement as simply making a
virtue of necessity. Transport exigencies decided how the
troops were to be deployed, and it was ridiculous to imag-
ine that the army of spies in Japan had not taken full note
of the size of the garrison there.

General Almond's description of the piecemeal commitment of troops differed sharply from MacArthur's. It was,
said Almond, his own recommendation. In a debriefing in
March 1975, by Captain Thomas Ferguson, a student at
the Command and General Staff School, Almond put it
simply—"It was the only thing we could do." The troops
were stripped of all equipment except side arms and were
carried by plane, assembled at Pusan and then moved
north "to the degree the enemy would permit."

The first troops committed consisted of a battalion of
the 21st Regiment of the 24th Division under Lieutenant
Colonel C. B. Smith and were named Task Force Smith.
They were selected solely because they were, at the very
moment, undergoing air-transportability training. When
they were sent off to stand against an enemy that outnum-

bered them by about a hundred to one, neither MacArthur nor anyone else on our side had any notion that the entire Eighth Army would soon have to follow. As he had blithely underestimated the Japanese forces that might attack the Philippines, MacArthur grossly misjudged the size, the spirit and the readiness of the North Korean forces; he had already accepted the idea that the ROK Constabulary, supposed to be a hundred thousand strong, was "the best doggoned shooting army outside the United States."

After visiting the battle front, just below the River Han, MacArthur assured Marguerite Higgins, the correspondent for the *New York Herald Tribune,* that he could stop the North Korean advance with two American divisions. In a matter of six days or less, his estimate and his requests to the Pentagon began to skyrocket, for if anyone had been "fooled" by his enemy, it was MacArthur himself. He must have been dismayed quite early to learn that, of the supposed hundred thousand ROKs who were to hold back the North Koreans, only eight thousand had been "found." A week later, another eight thousand were discovered. But not many of these or of the original force had any great desire to fight. (An exception was the ROK 6th Division, which stubbornly held off the NKPA for three days just north of Seoul.)

MacArthur and his sycophants bragged often that the brilliant tactics of the Commander in Chief forced the enemy to halt at the banks of the Han and deploy his artillery, for fear the American forces might be too strong for him to overcome by tanks and infantry alone. But if anything did slow down the North Koreans it was the skill and celerity of the Air Force in taking out the bridges over the Han and in destroying much of the enemy armor.

After they crossed the Han, nothing held the NKPA

back but the steaming courage of the weary, outnumbered, and outgunned men of the 24th Infantry Division, fighting without reserves, with almost no chance to sleep, and with weapons that wrought no more damage on the enemy armor than a hundred bean blowers might have. For seventeen days, without relief or reinforcement, short of proper ammunition, short of food, short of sleep, the 24th made seven desperate stands, while yielding seventy miles to the enemy.

And finally it was the aggressiveness and energy of the general that MacArthur most disliked—Walton Walker—that stopped the North Korean drive. Shifting his forces madly about as one emergency after another arose, Walker established a sort of line—really a series of strong points—where, according to one cynical soldier, "everybody had everybody else surrounded" and the Americans managed to hold a defensive position following the general line of the Naktong river.

When Walker's command post was at Taegu, about the first of August, MacArthur, on learning a withdrawal to Pusan was being planned, hastened to visit Walker and tell him he would issue no order for such a withdrawal. There will be no Goddamn Dunkirk in this command (or words to that effect), MacArthur told Walker. And Walker, whose own staff had obviously been urging retreat, walked into the staff meeting and told them, "This army fights where it stands!"

Walker then personally told his troops, "We are going to hold this line! We are going to win!"

In a recent letter, General John A. Dabney, Walker's operations officer, recalls that he was the one who protested, after he had drawn up at the behest of the Chief of Staff an order for a withdrawal to a shorter line around Pusan.

After the staff had labored all night on the complex plan, General Walker came by at five in the morning to see whether the plan was ready. Dabney urged that the order not be issued, as the ground would be needed if they were ever to stage an attack to break out of the perimeter. Walker agreed that they should hold fast.

(Both MacArthur and Walker, before the year was out, were making detailed plans for a phased withdrawal from Seoul to Pusan, where the command was to be withdrawn from the peninsula.)

By this time the 25th and the 1st Cavalry Division, which had been strengthened through the depletion of the 7th Division (still in Japan), had joined the battle. But this did not mean any letup for the battered and sleepless 24th. They were moved west and south to the Naktong to protect the left flank. By August 1, and just in time to avert disaster, Walker's forces were built up to near combat strength by the arrival of the Army's 5th Regimental Combat Team from Hawaii, the 2nd Infantry Division, and, one day later, the 1st Provisional Marine Brigade.

The major threat, at this point, was an enemy column moving down the west coast of the peninsula toward the naval base at Masan, threatening to cut off our forces before Pusan and bring on a massive slaughter when the scattered U.N. forces had to fight their way to safety.

Walker swiftly moved the 25th Division from the north and dispatched the Provisional Marine Brigade to the same sector. This Brigade included the 5th Marines, who brought M-26 Pershing tanks equipped with 90-mm. guns. For the first time we had a tank that would outmatch the enemy's T-34s. This was just force enough to tip the balance, to stop the North Korean advance dead and give Walker the time he needed to set up the line that became

the Pusan perimeter. Had a less resourceful and energetic
man been in command of Eighth Army at that point there
might never have been any Operation Chromite—the
MacArthur Miracle of Inchon—nor any cascades of glory
to celebrate the military genius of the man who did not
cringe at being named the Hero of Bataan.

MacArthur, not long after this gallant stand, was confid-
ing to associates that "I may have to relieve Walker." His
complaint was that Walker did not promptly break out of
the Pusan perimeter when the Inchon landing had been
announced. But there was a wide river facing Walker, with
an enemy on the other side still generously supplied, well
armed and full of fight. And Walker still had not received
the engineering equipment he had been begging for, to enable him to fight his way across the river. "We have been
bastard children," he told the GHQ in Tokyo. "But I don't
want you to think I have been dragging my heels." But
MacArthur had no ears for details.

Where MacArthur did show his brilliance and his special
gifts of eloquence and persuasiveness was in collating, cat-
aloguing and interpreting the half-ton of facts and figures
his staff compiled for him to illustrate that it really would
be possible to land a force at Inchon and destroy the North
Korean army between hammer and anvil. It is difficult for
a layman to agree, however, that the simple conception of
the idea—striking the enemy at a point where the enemy
"knew" no attack was possible, in the manner of Wolfe at
Quebec—required either soaring intelligence or transcendent powers of analysis. The general idea had been put
into practice countless times in the history of warfare, by
George Washington at Dorchester Heights, for instance,
and by the Japanese at Singapore.

What was necessary to make Inchon possible was the

assembling of a staff of military planners of exceptional skill and experience. In putting together such an assemblage, MacArthur was at his best. There probably never was a more talented array of naval and military experts gathered for one job than the group of men who planned Inchon. Nor was any general ever better briefed than MacArthur was when he took on the task of talking his superiors out of their conviction that an Inchon landing simply would not work. Men who had come to that meeting armed with facts and figures to support their contention were left speechless when MacArthur, right out of his amazing memory, recited their facts back to them—the tide tables at Inchon, the weather forecasts, the state and the strength of the defense force, the risks of allowing the enemy to dig in for the winter, the danger of open intervention by the Chinese or the Soviets.

First he had to persuade the President and the Joint Chiefs of Staff that his scheme would work swiftly enough to forestall any expansion of the war, that the risk was worth stripping the United States of a large part of its General Reserve, and that the planning had been careful enough to make success a real possibility. MacArthur called it a 5,000-to-1 gamble; but, of course, if the odds had been even nearly that wild, the Joint Chiefs would never have approved it.

As it was, when the first emissaries from the Pentagon, including Averell Harriman, personal representative of President Truman, General Larry Norstad, Vice-Chief of Staff of the Air Force, and Lieutenant General Matthew B. Ridgway, Deputy Army Chief of Staff, met in a two-hour conference with MacArthur and his own Chief of Staff, Major General Edward M. Almond, MacArthur completely won over the three skeptics from Washington—so

much so that they all returned full of enthusiasm for the
plan, and convinced that the dangers were too great to
postpone its immediate approval.

There was one rather ominous sidelight to that conference that no one made much of at the time. When someone
questioned MacArthur about the possibility that the Chinese might intervene, he replied: "I pray nightly that they
will—would get down on my knees."

Just why he should have yearned for any such major
disaster no one now can say. Averell Harriman believes
that MacArthur pictured the Chinese army as they were in
the days of the warlords, a mob of sullen, undisciplined and
poorly armed conscripts out of another century who would
have been mere cannon fodder for a modern army. But
surely this private hope that he might soon meet the Chinese Communists in battle must have influenced him in ignoring the directive to halt any advance into North Korea
if there was evidence of major Chinese intervention. It may
even have enabled him to justify to himself his refusal to
accept the clear evidence that major units in the Chinese
order of battle had already engaged his troops in Korea.

Disregarding directives and ignoring evidence that
might divert him from pursuing some private aim were
standard procedure for MacArthur. Dr. D. Clayton James,
in an article that appeared in *Parameters,* the official jour-
nal of the United States Army War College, in June 1980,
notes that MacArthur in 1945, a few weeks after a beachhead had been established on Luzon, sent the Eighth Army
to seize the rest of the Philippines without waiting for any
directive from the Joint Chiefs and in face of severe losses
being suffered by the Sixth Army in battles for strong
points on Luzon. And, despite the rejection by the Joint
Chiefs of his plan to invade Java, MacArthur still told
General Eichelberger that he planned to attack that island

if the "Navy idea of piddling around . . . carries through."
One writer for *Time* magazine, in July 1950, even seemed
to consider it one of the hero's virtues that he paid little
attention to the desires of his "nominal superiors."

Had the Java invasion ever been staged, the result would
have been, according to Dr. James, a "tragic bloodbath,"
for the island was far more heavily defended than Mac-
Arthur believed. Its strategic value at that stage of the war
was about zero, so MacArthur, instead of coming out as the
hero of the Pacific, might well have found his reputation
hopelessly damaged. Fortunately for everyone, the war
ended before MacArthur could commit this blunder. Yet,
typically, MacArthur, in his *Reminiscences* (or Whitney
speaking for him) tried to portray this as a great victory
that was denied him by jealous, shortsighted, or even trai-
torous figures at home. At the same time, he reveals what
some Australian commentators suspected, that his plans
were motivated more by political than by strategic considerations.

> After the Borneo campaign [MacArthur (or Whitney)
> writes] I had planned to proceed with the Australian troops
> to Java [with two Australian divisions!] and to retake the
> Netherlands East Indies. Then, as in New Guinea, restora-
> tion of the Dutch government would have brought the return
> of orderly administration and law. But for reasons I have
> never been able to discover, the proposed movement was
> summarily vetoed by Washington—even in the face of my as-
> surance that its full success was certain at minor cost. This
> reversal soon bore fruit in the chaos that ensued in that por-
> tion of Indonesia; it was a grave error and was the result of
> meddling in what was essentially a military matter.

There is something quite essentially MacArthurish in
that final statement, in which, after explaining his own po-

litical motives (to return the Dutch colonialists to power),
he names the move a military matter.

It is fortunate for MacArthur that he had working for
him at Inchon a number of able officers who had not been
infected by the Tokyo atmosphere. A few of those charged
with meeting the first thrusts of the North Koreans were
all too plainly, as General Michaelis said, unfit physically
or professionally to carry on under the rigors of combat.
Marguerite Higgins, in her book *War in Korea,* describes a
scene at Suwon, temporary American headquarters during
the withdrawal from Seoul to Pusan, when one officer
rushed into headquarters shouting "We're surrounded!
We're surrounded!" setting off a wild rush for the airfield
by the officers, with no concern for the safety of the troops.
As it turned out, they were not surrounded at all. Perhaps
they had simply adopted the philosophy of some anonymous rhymester in World War II:

> When in danger, when in doubt
> Run in circles! Scream and shout!

Elsewhere there was gallantry aplenty among officers
and men. And there was bitterness, fear, even despair.
Time magazine quoted one lieutenant who had survived
the fighting on the retreat to Pusan—a man who had seen
heavy combat during World War II—"I don't claim to understand the grand strategy of this thing, but I will never
again lead men into a situation like that one. We were ordered to hold at all costs. We did but the cost was awful!"

Lieutenant Junior Childers from California reported the
efforts of his company to get into position to slow the
NKPA advance:

"They split my company before we could get into the
fight. It was a slaughterhouse! They mounted machine
guns on the hills above us and swept us clean. Then they

threw 20-millimeter bursts around us. Below us the tanks
opened up. Nine men dropped around me and I brought
out three."

Still, total casualties in the fighting were not nearly so
high as platoon-level reports made them sound. The
American forces were overwhelmingly outnumbered, and
often the NKPA just swept ahead without opposition.

But more than one American was outraged to see trainloads of ROKs, that "best doggoned shooting army," fully
armed and equipped, rolling southward away from the
battle. MacArthur, who had scolded the correspondents a
few days earlier for reporting the fall of Seoul and described such stories as "war hysteria," also assured them
that the South Korean army needed only to be rallied
"with examples and leadership." They were able to view
the examples from their train windows but obviously did
not profit by them. As for leadership, that had been imposed on them by the Rhee government, with MacArthur's
blessing.

The Chief of Staff of the South Korean Army was a
monstrous character named Choi Lyung Duk, who had
served as a major in the Japanese army and consequently
was looked on as a traitor by the run-of-the-mill Korean.
He weighed three hundred pounds and bulged out alarm-
ingly all around his chair. Koreans used to laugh at his frequent promises, before the war began, and often delivered
through the mouth of Syngman Rhee, that if he were given
the order in Seoul at nine in the morning, he could drive
his troops through North Korea and eat a victory supper
that night in Sinuiju, on the Manchurian border.

"How would he ever make the trip?" some disrespectful
young Koreans used to ask. "If he got into a jeep, there'd
be no room for the driver."

It was not that the plain Korean had no love for his

country or lacked desire to serve, or that he was sympathetic to Communism. But the soldiers in the ROK army
were stingily paid, fed about half what they needed, and
wretchedly clothed. Money for equipment, like the money
sent from America to transport, feed, clothe and house the
horde of refugees, was routinely misappropriated by the
army officers and the countless bureaucrats in the Rhee
regime. Korean soldiers had no respect whatever for their
superiors, who having nothing in common with the plain
people, held their jobs only because of their political con-
nections. Men who had been awarded commissions in
Rhee's army were constantly looking to feather their own
nests, imbued as they were with the Rhee philosophy that
government and military jobs provided the easiest route to
status and good living. A few soldiers, however, did earn
advancement in the army through being selected by some
superior officer because of their fluency in English and skill
with a typewriter to act as secretary and interpreter. These
men, scornfully named "swallows" by the soldiers in the
ranks, were rewarded by never seeing combat.

MacArthur related in his book that he partly solved the
problem of getting the Koreans to fight by installing a
"buddy" system, under which a hundred or so Korean conscripts were awarded to each American company for integration in every platoon. But platoon leaders who had experience with giving orders to men who could not
understand a word that was said to them, failed to share
his enthusiasm. Even General Almond, MacArthur's Chief
of Staff, expressed doubts about this system. The Koreans
involved were not soldiers but refugees swept up off the
streets of Pusan, bewildered, hungry, ragged and scared.
Most of the troops of the 7th Infantry Division, still in
Japan, although it had been gutted to beef up the units of

the Eighth Army that were already in action, were used as instructors to train the nine thousand conscripts in infantry squad duties. Many of the GIs, and officers too, who considered the Koreans a lesser breed, referred to them freely as "gooks," and sneered to see them mistaking toothpaste for something good to eat and wearing one uniform over another to make sure of holding on to it. Poverty that deep was clearly un-American. Why, you even had to show them how to use a latrine!

Despite his success with the men from the Pentagon, MacArthur did not find it quite so easy to persuade the men who were to be charged with staging the Inchon landing that it was entirely feasible. For one thing his Army planners, who would not take over command until all the troops had been put ashore and outfitted, were inclined to look on an amphibious operation as, in General Almond's phrase, "a simple mechanical problem." The Navy men had made solemn note of the fact that the "beaches" chosen for the various landings were not beaches at all. "Green Beach" was a strip on the northwest shore of Wolmi-do, the island that commanded the harbor, and it consisted of rocks with patches of sand. "Red Beach" was about 200 yards of sea wall, reaching north from the causeway connecting Wolmi-do to the mainland. Ladders would be needed to scale it. "Blue Beach" was the area south of Inchon, again lined with sea walls, backed by salt pans and mud flats. So there were many questions unanswered.

How high were the sea walls? Would the mudflats support a man? A vehicle? And how many of the observed gun emplacements actually held guns? How heavily fortified was Wolmi-do? Were the channels mined?

These were some of the "details" that General Almond tried to keep MacArthur from being troubled with. Indeed, the Army planners had laid out their plans almost as if the landing were a closed question and the real problem was how to get to Seoul from the beach. Luckily Vice-Admiral Doyle had his way, and the Navy and Marine planners were able to add their own experience and expertise to the general fund. Vice-Admiral Doyle and Lieutenant General Oliver Smith of the Marine Corps never were wholly convinced that Inchon was the best choice for the landing. It was Doyle's premise that almost any landing was possible and that the important matter was the price in lives. A landing a few miles south of Inchon, Doyle always maintained, could have achieved the same result at small cost in human life.

Admiral Doyle many years later had still not forgotten his irritation, during a briefing for MacArthur, General J. Lawton Collins, and Admiral Forrest P. Sherman, when his description of the formidable difficulties facing the task force, with enemy shore batteries completely controlling the dead-end channel, was interrupted by Admiral Sherman, who vowed, in a ringing tone: "*I* would not hesitate to take a ship up there!"

"Spoken like a Farragut!" MacArthur responded.

"Spoken like a John Wayne!" Admiral Doyle told himself. It took him, he allowed later, five to ten years to cool off after that.

Doyle finally did get an agreement that allowed him at least one day, and if need be, two, to knock out the guns that might have wrecked the whole enterprise. And, he confessed, he had his own John Wayne-ish moment when MacArthur assured him, after Doyle had voiced his doubts, that if the project proved impossible they could withdraw. "No," said Doyle. "We don't know how to do that."

As it turned out, of course, withdrawal never had to be

considered, but Doyle and General Smith had many a moment after that to writhe at the workings of the minds of MacArthur and his surrogates. Schemes were brewed for ventures, sometimes including General Smith's own forces, that would have one landing force climbing right up the backs of another or a company of commandos in rubber boats fighting against impossible tides, then floundering over half a mile of mud flats, out of touch with their own forces, vulnerable to friendly naval guns, against an enemy force four times as strong. When the folly of this venture had finally caused its cancellation, General Almond, as reported by Colonel Robert D. Heinl, Jr., in his excellent book *Victory at High Tide,* explained that he had supported this scheme to "spur on the Marines." Just as if the Marines, the most aggressive and best-led forces in the operation, needed to be goosed into performing their assigned task. Said Smith, "He didn't understand Marines."

Possibly even more irritating to the rank and file who did the fighting was the triumphant announcement by General Almond (who sometimes, according to Admiral Doyle, got himself confused with MacArthur), just before midnight on September 25, that Seoul had been liberated. The fact was that there were three more days of fierce close-up combat ahead, with the NKPA defenders contesting every street corner.

This sort of premature announcement was no novelty at MacArthur headquarters. In World War II, on January 8, 1943, MacArthur himself had announced to the world, "The Papuan campaign is in its final closing phase. The Sanananda position has now been completely enveloped. A remnant of the enemy's forces is entrenched there and faces certain destruction. With it, Papua will be entirely cleared of the enemy. . . ."

Actually, there were seven thousand Japanese (almost half the original force) dug in around Sanananda, and two weeks of some of the bitterest fighting of the campaign still lay ahead.

In Davao too, MacArthur reported that "strategic victory" had been "achieved" when many weeks of the toughest fighting remained. At Buna, MacArthur's communiqué on Christmas 1942, told the world that "our activities were limited to routine safety precautions. Divine services were held." But General Robert Eichelberger, who was on the scene, while MacArthur was leagues away, wrote that on Christmas "the fighting was desperate and the outcome of the whole miserable tortured campaign was in doubt."

It was after Seoul had really been cleared of the enemy and the "pursuit phase" of the war was about to begin, that MacArthur made what a number of his colleagues, including Admiral Doyle, still consider one of his most egregious blunders, from motives that still seem obscure. With the Eighth Army now running short of all vital supplies, particularly artillery shells, but including gasoline, clothing and bridging material, MacArthur ordered X Corps to be withdrawn through the port of Inchon, in order that he might repeat the Inchon miracle on the opposite coast, at Wonsan, a North Korean port well above the 38th parallel. This meant that the Inchon port facilities would be choked with traffic as troops and equipment of X Corps, selected to engage in this amphibious operation, were off-loaded and all supplies to Eighth Army would be instantly cut off. To MacArthur it may have seemed another simple mechanical operation, just putting a lot of soldiers on ships to carry them around to be landed on the opposite coast. But Admiral Doyle, who was perhaps the ablest man in the Navy in managing amphibious operations, could have told him differently. It was going to be one hell of a job, Doyle knew, for he was still unloading equipment and supplies for the 1st Marine Division. Now he had to embark the whole division in the configuration for an over-the-beach combat landing, a task that required highly specialized knowledge and minute attention to detail.

There was no excess shipping available. Every square inch of cargo space had to be used efficiently and in the proper sequence, lest landing forces be deprived of essential equipment when they needed it most. And, of course, the completion of this job meant that there was a long stoppage of incoming supplies for the Eighth Army, still actively engaged with the enemy. All rail traffic from Seoul to Pusan also had to be given over at once to the job of moving X Corps on this mission that one military observer later referred to as an instance of MacArthur's "faulty handling of troops."

Doyle and several Army officers agreed that the swiftest, the most efficient and the obvious way to move X Corps to Wonsan was under the control of Eighth Army, and by land along the railroad and the existing highway from Seoul to Wonsan. No one can say, of course, exactly why MacArthur made this decision. There were sound military reasons for seizing Wonsan (provided that the United Nations had authorized, or would authorize, a crossing of the 38th parallel). Wonsan was the most important naval base in North Korea, and the principal port on the west coast. Russian supplies for the North Korean army came through Wonsan from Vladivostok, and it was the major petroleum-refining center in North Korea, as well as a rail center and the terminus of a good highway across the peninsula to the North Korean capital of Pyongyang. And there were apparently sound reasons advanced for avoiding the overland route; there were indications that the route, through rugged mountains, would be heavily defended. And to try to supply both X Corps and Eighth Army through Inchon might have created a disastrous tangle. Major General Edwin K. Wright, who took part in the discussions preceding this move, still feels the decision was proper.

But not, according to a high Pentagon official, if X Corps had been allowed to come immediately under control of Eighth Army. To try to keep it as a separate command, to be controlled from General Headquarters eight hundred miles away, seemed the utmost folly. The decision seems even stranger in the light of what General Almond recalled at his debriefing twenty-five years later. According to Almond, when he protested at being put in charge of the land forces at Inchon, because he did not feel he could do that job properly and remain as Chief of Staff, MacArthur assured him, "Well, we'll all be home by Christmas, and therefore it is only a short operation and the Eighth Army will become the controlling factor as soon as we capture the port of entry."

After a remark like this, to take such extreme pains to separate X Corps from General Walker's command could almost be characterized as pathological. Admiral Doyle suspects that the well-known bitterness between Almond and Walker, with MacArthur, of course, privately taking the part of his Chief of Staff (and all-time favorite), really prompted this separation. Almond no doubt would have suffered great discomfort under the immediate direction of a man he disliked so intensely. But back at the Pentagon there were cynical souls, all anonymous, who named this whole operation, including the eventual drive to the Yalu,

"Operation Three-Star," meaning that it was an elaborate design to help MacArthur's white-haired boy earn a promotion to lieutenant general.

MacArthur has been accused, by men in a position to judge, of staging military operations or running needless risks for reasons every bit as personal as that. His moving Eighth Army, in World War II, from Luzon to Mindanao, leaving Eichelberger's Sixth Army short of strength while still engaged in a desperate struggle with the Japanese, has been ascribed by some, as the historian Dr. D. Clayton James points out, to MacArthur's urgent desire to make possible, through the liberation of more pro-Roxas voting strength, the election of his friend Manuel Roxas to the presidency of the Philippines—thus ensuring MacArthur's own future as highly paid Field Marshal of the Philippine Army. And years earlier MacArthur suddenly found room on what was supposed to be a dangerously overcrowded escape submarine, to take President Quezon and Mrs. Quezon safely away from Corregidor after Quezon had paid him a half-million-dollar "reward" for his services to the Philippine nation. This episode came to light in February 1979, when Dr. Carol Morris Petillo, an assistant professor of history at Boston College, published an article about it in the *Pacific Historical Review*.

MacArthur's dream of another Inchon (if that is what he envisioned when he chose to take Wonsan by means of an amphibious operation) evaporated quickly when the Marines arrived in Wonsan harbor (after minesweepers had spent days clearing it of mines) and found that the ROK I Corps pursuing the disorganized NKPA forces up the east coast, had already taken over the port. The Marines then made an "administrative" landing—meaning that not a shot was fired in anger. But a large part of the retreating

North Koreans had escaped into the mountains, when they might have been cut off, had Walker been allowed to drive overland to Wonsan.

What happened next is the most controversial of all the moves MacArthur made in Korea, the action that prompted some of his most embarrassing falsehoods and resulted in many scenes so disgraceful, from a professional soldier's point of view, that men who were engaged in them still cannot talk about them without bitterness. MacArthur's disdain for "detail" and his ability to close his eyes to unpleasant developments played a large part therein.

In the first place, there was the matter of Chinese intervention. Chinese broadcasts had been steadily repeating the vow that the Chinese were not going to sit idly by if the United Nations forces undertook to invade a friendly neighbor. Many listeners on the scene accepted these threats as mere bluster, typical of Communist air talk. There was even a widespread fairy tale, devoutly believed by many a GI, that MacArthur had sent an emissary to Mao Tse-tung with bags of gold and bribed him into staying out of the conflict. (There had to be some overpowering and top-secret basis, the GIs reasoned, for MacArthur's serene conviction that the Chinese would never intervene.) MacArthur said nothing, at this point, about his prayers that the Chinese would enter the war, but he did aver that, should they come in, air power would demolish them at the border and corpses would be piled six deep or so. And no Chinese general "in his right mind," he declared, would risk a fate like *that*.

The first evidence of Chinese intervention was not a trifling one. The 7th Regiment of the ROK 6th Division, which had actually reached the Yalu river, bordering Manchuria, was struck without warning by an overwhelming force of Chinese that very nearly wiped out the regiment. At about the same time, but far to the east, another ROK force, meeting strong resistance, took eighteen prisoners from two different regiments of the Chinese 124th Division. And when the Marines arrived a few days later to relieve the ROK troops, they met and destroyed Chinese tanks and took a prisoner from still another Chinese Division, the 126th. Both the 124th and 126th Divisions belonged to the Chinese Forty-second Army.

Despite this live evidence, the MacArthur headquarters in Tokyo continued to assure Washington that there was no "firm indication" whatever of Chinese intervention, and that they did not believe that any more than a few Chinese volunteers had actually crossed the border.

This bland refusal to accept living proof irritated many of the corps and division commanders who were charged with pressing forward into areas where they felt sure strong enemy forces awaited them. Lieutenant General Frank Milburn, commanding I Corps, determined to present some solid evidence to awaken his superiors to the fact that there *were* live Chinese on the battleground, once sent an aid, Lieutenant Colonel John Austin, to pick up and bring back a Chinese prisoner reported taken on his front. Austin drove out and took delivery of the handcuffed man—a gigantic fellow obviously in the grip of fear—placed him in the jeep beside him and started back to corps headquarters. Along the way, Austin had to stop to relieve himself. He ordered his big prisoner out of the jeep first and the man promptly fell to his knees on the ground, jabbering in a high-pitched voice, apparently convinced he was about to be shot and begging for mercy. When he saw suddenly what Austin's real purpose was, he laughed happily and offered a number of indecipherable comments, which seemed to be expressions of willingness to be friends.

But the prisoner was turned over to the intelligence division and nothing more was heard. There was *still* no Chinese intervention, as far as GHQ was concerned.

As for detail, particularly of terrain and weather, MacArthur showed no interest. It first had made sense of a sort that, if X Corps was to operate along the east coast, it should come under separate control, as the intervening mountain range that would divide General Walker's Eighth Army from X Corps as they advanced was so high in places (ranging over 6,000 feet) that even direct radio communication was often impossible and physical liaison a nightmare. Yet when Walker suggested that the ROK II Corps on his right flank, already positioned on the overland route to Wonsan, should push on to that city and link up with the ROK I Corps so that, with the seizure of Pyongyang, he could extend a line across the peninsula from Wonsan, MacArthur, according to the account in General Matthew Ridgway's book *The Korean War,* "curtly refused." Instead, MacArthur informed Walker that, once the Marines had cleared the mines and landed, ROK I Corps would be taken from Walker's command and come under the command of X Corps. And, to make Walker's lot even more unbearable, MacArthur charged Walker with logistical support of X Corps troops as well as his own. In MacArthur's mind, obviously, the geographical barriers did not exist. As a matter of fact, after abandoning his original plan for a two-pronged advance up the peninsula, MacArthur sent his forces along wildly separate routes toward the Yalu—not only ignoring the directive from the Joint Chiefs of Staff that he should use only native troops in border areas or even areas close to the border, but calmly ignoring the terrain.

The only way these scattered forces could have maintained ground contact with each other, let alone offer mutual support, was if the mountains over which they ranged did not exist. They were just more details that MacArthur had no mind for. The men in the Pentagon, however, were dismayed by this helter-skelter dispersal. And when, in justifying himself before the Senate some time later, MacArthur declared, "Had I known of the enemy's presence in force I could not have better disposed my troops," well, some who knew that MacArthur was master enough in military science to know better, privately called him a liar.

But more shocking falsehoods were those MacArthur told to exculpate himself when his blunders led the U.N. forces to disaster. More about this in later chapters.

3

small lies

General Horatio Gates, commanding general of the American forces at the greatest victory of our own Revolution, the defeat of the British at Saratoga, said afterward that the "great tacticians of the campaign were hills and forests." What he meant, of course, was that brilliant use of the terrain forced the British to press their attack in such a way as to ensure their defeat. And the man who turned the terrain into a weapon was a Polish colonel whose name even George Washington never could pronounce properly, Thaddeus Kosciuszko, a military genius who not only brought victory at Saratoga but, by careful placement of fortifications, prevented the siege of Philadelphia and kept the British fleet out of the upper Hudson. Kosciuszko, whose accomplishments were lucidly set forth in a fine article by Major Ernest L. Cuneo in the July 1978 issue of *Officer Review,* was, however, a studiously self-effacing man whose fame, unlike MacArthur's, quickly faded, prompting no fulsome biographies nor public monuments.

Still, MacArthur, who was given to intense study of military history, would have done well to spend some time with Kosciuszko. He would have learned at least that no man should deem himself a master strategist who gives as scant consideration to terrain as MacArthur did in Korea. With no more knowledge of where he was deploying his forces than he might have gathered from a quick glance at a map, MacArthur ordered X Corps and Eighth Army off toward the Yalu on his end-the-war offensive and blandly predicted that they would bring hostilities to an end in a matter of weeks. Forces that were supposed to be mutually supporting could not even signal each other on their field radios. Roads over which armor was supposed to advance turned out either not to exist or to be hardly more than footpaths through mountains so high not even a goat could scale them. But, as GIs in Korea were given to reminding each other, "Nothing moves faster than a grease pencil on a sheet of warm acetate."

Troops in summer clothing, with nothing more substantial to warm them than windbreaker-type jackets, were sent to fight through freezing streams and waist-deep snow. Front-line troops on the advance saw no hot food and indeed had to tuck their C rations under their arms at night so the food would not be frozen solid in the morning. Major General Oliver P. Smith, commanding the 1st Marine Division, was fully aware that the ROK II Corps, which was supposed to offer some sort of protection to his left flank (although seventy miles away!), had suddenly collapsed under Chinese assault; so he moved his forces with sensible caution along the only road toward his objective. But he was constantly prodded by General Almond at X Corps headquarters to speed up his advance. Even twenty-five years later, Almond complained about General Smith, that he was "overly cautious of executing any order he ever received" and that "while he never refused to obey an order in the final analysis, he many times was overcautious and in that way delayed the execution of some orders."

The fact was that had not Smith been "overly cautious" and had he not, as he dutifully reported to headquarters, taken "every feasible measure to develop and guard the Main Supply Route" and ensured that at all times he had "possession of the high ground along the route of the division's advance," the whole division might well have been destroyed. And had he not, resisting the constant importunities from higher up, taken the time to prepare an airstrip at the south end of Changjin reservoir, for supply and for the removal of wounded, his troops could never have extricated themselves from the Chinese trap.

When the Chinese did strike, not just in the area where the Marine forward elements were positioned, but even far to the west, where the Eighth Army was supposed to be pushing rapidly toward the Yalu, MacArthur and Almond did not hesitate to declare—after the true extent of the debacle became clear—that they had expected some such thing and had made preparations for orderly withdrawal. Almond in his 1975 debriefing even asserted that General Smith's mission had been to "press forward and determine what, if any, and how much Chinese force there was in my front. . . ." But General Smith's orders, as recorded by General Ridgway in his book *The Korean War,* had been to "advance up on the roof of Korea north and northwest to Kanggye and Manpojin on the Yalu." And if this movement had been a "reconnaissance in force," as MacArthur described it afterward, would any sensible commander, not to suggest a "great strategist," have committed his entire reserve to the venture, as MacArthur did?

General Walker too was sharply prodded by General
Headquarters for his slowness in advancing across the
Chongchon river to the border and became convinced just
before he died that he was about to be relieved of his job—
because of the retreat that he and General Smith had
known all along might well become necessary. For Walker,
disturbed by the growing gap, as the peninsula widened
between his forces and X Corps, also took care while moving forward to make preparations for retirement. Without
such preparations, General Ridgway writes, he might well
have lost most of his army.

In 1975, General Almond, who was never cited for open-
mindedness, still insisted that the advance to the Yalu was
in the nature of a probe to discover the strength of the Chinese and that there was logic in the disposition of the
troops, with the 1st Marine Division protecting the right
flank of Eighth Army and the 7th Infantry Division, advancing toward Hyesanjin on the Yalu, protecting the
right flank of the Marines. According to General Ridgway,
however, the 7th Infantry Division had to move northwest
along a narrow dirt-and-gravel pathway as steep and sin-
uous as the road taken by the Marines. "Between these
forces," Ridgway writes, "there was nothing but impass-
able mountain country, making mutual support impossible
and preventing even patrol contact." And between Eighth
Army and 1st Marine Division there were well over seventy miles of towering and often unscalable cliffs.

In the face of heated denials by MacArthur and his court
that MacArthur had ever even suggested that this advance
would end the war and that they would all be "home by
Christmas," it is well to look at the record as noted at the
time. To begin with, there was the famous Wake Island
conference, which itself has given rise to fairy tales from

both sides of the controversy, some of which have already
jelled into history. Of minor importance is the story invented by President Truman—a sort of fish story such as
old men will "remember," particularly if memory has been
brightened by drink and embellished by a hunger for approval. For despite Truman's recollection of that jockeying
in the air to see which plane would land first, the President's or the General's, no such scene ever developed, nor
could it have, for the planes of the President's party according to Averell Harriman, who flew in one of them, arrived a good twelve hours after the General's. The scolding
and the angry finger-shaking that Truman "remembered"
never took place. When MacArthur met Truman's plane, it
is true, he studiously avoided saluting the President although he had been in the Army long enough to realize
that the President was his military superior. But otherwise
the meeting was cordial. There were no angry words exchanged at any time. Truman awarded MacArthur his fifth
Distinguished Service Medal, and each expressed delight
at meeting the other.

Ambassador Muccio accompanied the General to Wake
Island, although he might not have done so if he had not
previously received a mysterious message from Secretary
Dean Rusk that said simply "If invited, accept." Muccio
had no idea what this might mean until there arrived soon
afterward a message from Air Force General Earle Partridge that the General had instructions to "have you at
Haneda Airport at 11 A.M. if you want." Muccio never felt
he was a subordinate of MacArthur's. He had received a
few testy radio messages from MacArthur when he had
sent some plain-spoken advice to MacArthur about the
dispatch of a U.S. destroyer to "rescue" a Japanese fishing
boat seized by the Korean Coast Guard. Speaking of the

abrupt message from Partridge long afterward, Muccio chuckled, "If it hadn't been for that message from Rusk I'd have told him to go to hell."

MacArthur, on the flight, Muccio recalled, was "surly, uneasy, and mad." MacArthur was always uneasy about flying, although he sometimes made a show of being sound asleep during a flight. This time he sat on the edge of his seat or paced up and down the aisle, complaining about being called away from his duties when he had "a war to fight." His demeanor generally was that of a man heading against his will into a very unpleasant interview.

The interview was not unpleasant at all, although exactly what took place in the first talk, at which only the President and the General were present, is known only to the participants, and neither one was immune from the temptation to exaggerate or even falsify. Of the general conference that followed in the weather shack, MacArthur's recollection is amazingly self-serving. In his *Reminiscences,* he recalls that there was nothing discussed on which his views were not already known, until the very end, when, almost casually, the question of Chinese intervention was raised. According to MacArthur, he told the assemblage that his answer "could only be speculative." Then, he says, he explained that it was up to the State Department and the Central Intelligence Agency to divine Chinese intent and they had already advanced the opinion that the Chinese would not intervene. This, MacArthur recalled in his book, was the "general consensus of all present." As for himself, he told the group that his own local intelligence "reported heavy concentrations near the Yalu border in Manchuria whose movements were indeterminate." And all he ever said about what he might do to meet this threat was that considering "our largely unopposed air forces, with their potential capable of destroying at will, bases of attack and lines of supply *north as well as south of the Yalu* [my emphasis], no Chinese military commander would hazard the commitment of large forces . . ." MacArthur also recalled that General Omar Bradley even "went so far as to bring up the question of transferring troops in the Far East to Europe and said he would like to have two divisions home from Korea by Christmas for this purpose."

Thus, poor General Bradley (whom MacArthur once referred to as "a farmer") gets the blame for the "home by Christmas" slogan, even though General Almond could remember MacArthur's using those words to him just before Inchon.

Notes taken at the conference indicate clearly that MacArthur's later version was almost completely invented well after the fact. But the taking of these notes was itself characterized by MacArthur's devotees as an underhanded bit of eavesdropping. Others who were present all agree, however, that there was nothing secretive about the procedure at all.

The lady who took the notes, Vernice Anderson, secretary to U.N. Ambassador Philip Jessup, later was introduced to General MacArthur and, according to John Muccio, the fact that she had taken notes was explained. It certainly could not have shocked anyone to know that the minutes of this historic meeting had been taken down in shorthand. The MacArthur faithful and MacArthur himself suggested that she was "hidden" behind a door. But others who were there, including Ambassador Muccio, all agreed that she sat in plain sight of many people in the room, in a short hallway or alcove between the tiny meeting room and the room adjoining.

William Manchester, in *American Caesar,* even goes so

far as to write that the room "was bugged," as if the conference had actually been an elaborate trap to draw and
record from MacArthur some incriminating admission, and
that therefore, the non-MacArthur version was suspect.
But Averell Harriman in a telephone talk in 1980 recalled
the conference and the presence of Miss Anderson. "There
was not a single unfriendly word uttered!" he insisted.
"And anyway, why should she record something that did
not happen?"

One of the most detailed reports of the meeting is given
in a lively book *Silent Missions* by Brigadier General (then
Major) Vernon Walters, former Deputy Director of the
CIA, who came to Wake as an assistant to Averell Harriman. And the divergence between his version and the version offered by MacArthur in *Reminiscences* is total.
Walters, who sat right in the room with the conferees, and
took his own notes, says flatly that Truman asked Mac-
Arthur, not "casually" but as the very first question put to
the General after the briefing, whether the Chinese would
enter the war. And MacArthur, Walters writes, "speaking
slowly and dramatically," replied in these words: "Mr.
President, they will not enter this war. This is the hour of
our strength, not of our weakness. We no longer stand hat in
hand. If the Chinese Communists cross the Yalu, I shall make
of them the greatest slaughter in the history of mankind."

Averell Harriman, who took part in the conference, but
did not make notes, remembers MacArthur's statement
this way: "I *know* the Chinese will not intervene. If they
do, it will be one of the greatest slaughters in history.
Corpses will be piled six deep."

John Muccio, in a private conversation with MacArthur
on the plane going to the Wake Island meeting, recalls
MacArthur's telling him that nothing was left of the war
but "mop-up operations" and that "no organized enemy

remains." About three and a half hours after the meeting, MacArthur said to Muccio, "The Chinese may have 25,000. They can't possibly have more than 30,000." Actually, there were already more than ten times that number in Korea. Muccio blames Colonel Charles Willoughby, Mac-Arthur's German-born intelligence officer (who idolized Francisco Franco) for providing MacArthur with this sort of "intelligence." Willoughby (real name Tscheppe-Wei-denbach) did have a report from a Chinese agent in Hong Kong concerning Chinese strength in Manchuria. In September 1950 he passed a memo to MacArthur informing him that "it is probable the numerous reports of large-scale movements of Chinese Communist forces northward from Canton were actually Koreans, Manchurian-Koreans, and ex-Japanese troops being transferred to Manchuria and Korea." Willoughby noted that the presence of Chinese-trained Koreans in North Korea had already been confirmed and that there had been about 140,000 Koreans integrated with Chinese forces during the war against Chiang as well as some 25,000 Japanese serving with the artillery and other units requiring technical skill. This would indicate, said Willoughby, "about 165,000 troops deployed along Korean border." And Willoughby's opinion was that "rather than enter the war as active participants, it is probable that the Chinese Communists, if called upon, would furnish replacements through discreet integration into Korean units."

Whether MacArthur clung to this information to sustain his delusion that captives definitely identified as members of units in the Chinese order of battle were merely random volunteers cannot be known. He apparently never found it difficult to come up with "facts" to confirm whatever he wanted to believe.

MacArthur in Manila at the end of World War II. His eyes are on distant goals, one of which, as it turned out, was the Presidency of the United States.

Colonel (now General) Paul L. Freeman, Jr., who commanded the 23d Regimental Combat Team at Chipyong-ni, one of the most fiercely fought battles in Korea and one of the most important victories.

Lieutenant Colonel Johnny Austin, Secretary to the General Staff of I Corps and commander of an infantry regiment in Korea, brought one of the first Chinese prisoners back to Corps headquarters. He was present when MacArthur, in November 1950, made his "home-by-Christmas" promise.

John H. Michaelis earned a battlefield promotion from colonel to brigadier general in the fighting on the Pusan perimeter when he moved his forces, without waiting for orders, to stem an enemy breakthrough that threatened collapse of the perimeter defenses. This formal portrait was taken after the war when he was Commandant of the Cadet Corps at the U.S.M.A.

U.S. MILITARY ACADEMY ARCHIVES

General Matthew B. Ridgway, who took over command of the Eighth Army on the death of General Walton Walker and turned a defeated and demoralized army into a spirited fighting force. The grenade hooked to his harness is live.

U.S. ARMY PHOTOGRAPH

Brigadier General John A. Dabney, shown here accepting congratulations from General Ridgway on receiving the Distinguished Service Cross, was largely instrumental in the decision to yield no more ground at the Pusan perimeter.

General John Hodge at Fort Monroe, Virginia, on his return, health failing, from command of the U.S. armed forces in Korea before the war began. He told associates: "It was the worst job I ever had."

Major General Courtney Whitney, closest confidant and later biographer of General MacArthur.

MacArthur aboard the U.S.S. *Rochester* before the Inchon landing, talking with Brigadier-General Courtney Whitney, General Field Harris, U.S.M.C., and Vice-Admiral James H. Doyle, who directed the landing.

Lieutenant General Walton H. (Johnny) Walker, commander of the Eighth Army at the outbreak of the Korean War, who was killed in a jeep accident after the withdrawal from the Yalu. At the Pusan perimeter, he had told his troops: "This army fights where it stands!"

Major General Charles A. Willoughby, known to his subordinates as "the Prince." Born in Germany, and originally named Karl Tscheppe-Weidenbach, he was Mac-Arthur's intelligence officer.

Lieutenant General Edward M. Almond, MacArthur's Chief of Staff and commanding officer of X Corps at Inchon and on the advance to the Yalu. He earned his third star on that advance, despite the disaster that befell his forces there.

Syngman Rhee, who became the first president of the Republic of Korea, a country he had not seen for thirty years.

President Harry Truman and General MacArthur met for the first time on Wake Island in October 1950. Despite the stories that have since arisen, not an unpleasant word was exchanged between them.

In talking to his subordinates, MacArthur was both confident and convincing. Colonel John Austin recalls a meeting at the command post of I Corps some twenty miles below the Yalu in October, when MacArthur appeared before the entire Corps staff "erect and supremely confident. Absolutely at his peak, with an aura all around him." It was, said Austin, like watching "walking history," and the staff sat in silent awe as MacArthur calmly, quietly, punctuating each phrase with a poke of his cane, declared: "Gentlemen, the war is over. The Chinese are not coming into this war. In less than two weeks the Eighth Army will close on the Yalu across the entire front. The 3rd Division will be back at Fort Benning for Christmas dinner." Nobody questioned this, Austin recalls. "It would have been like questioning an announcement from God."

Yet MacArthur, in referring to this declaration after the debacle, said it had been made "jocularly." Strange to say, no one had laughed.

Perhaps the closest thing to a joke anyone can recall was MacArthur's message to General John Church of the 24th Division in late November of 1950, when there were nearly a half million Chinese troops in North Korea: "I have already promised the wives and mothers that the boys of the 24th Division will be back by Christmas. Don't make a liar of me. Get to the Yalu and I will relieve you." MacArthur, however, needed no help from anyone in making him a liar in this instance. His own words convict him.

Here is the communiqué (MacArthur called it communeek") from General Headquarters in Tokyo distributed by General Almond to his troops on November 24, 1950:

> The UN massive compression envelopment in North Korea against the new Red Armies operating there is now approaching its decisive effort. The isolating component of

the pincer, our air forces of all types, have for the past 3
weeks, in a sustained attack of model coordination and effec-
tiveness, successfully interdicted enemy lines of support from
the North so that further reinforcement therefrom has been
sharply curtailed and essential supplies markedly limited.
The Eastern sector of the pincer, with noteworthy and effective naval support, has steadily advanced in a brilliant tactical movement and has now reached a commanding envel-
oping position, cutting in two the northern reaches of the
enemy's geographical potential. This morning the Western
sector of the pincer moves forward in a general assault to
complete the compression and close the vise. If successful,
this should for all practical purposes end the war, restore
peace and unity to Korea, enable the prompt withdrawal of
the United Nations military forces and permit the complete
assumption by the Korean people and nation of full sov-
ereignty and international equality. It is that for which we
fight. [Signed] Douglas MacArthur, Commander-in-Chief.

To find jocularity in that message would require a funny
bone sized well above the average. And to read in it any
hint that the movement was intended as a reconnaissance
in force would be possible only to eyes blinded by hero
worship.

The diary kept by General Almond during his term as
commanding general of X Corps contains not the slightest
hint that the northward movement of the Corps was
merely a probe to "spring the trap" (MacArthur's words)
set by the not-sufficiently wily Chinese.

Here are the diary entries dated November 10, 1950:

1020: Arrived Yonghung and conferred with Colonel
Harris about movement of bn [battalion] to west. Movement
of this bn had not been energetic due to misinformation on

bridges and more speed was directed in order to provide means for contacting 8th Army on Corps-Army boundary.

1400: Arrived Pukchon and was briefed by the staff of 7th Inf. Div. CG X Corps (Almond) explained overall situation and the Corps scheme of maneuver i.e. to push the X Corps to the North Korean border.

The next diary entry, dated November 12, dealt with Almond's meeting with Joe DiMaggio and Lefty O'Doul, the touring baseball players.

Moving that battalion to the west to hook up with Eighth Army would have been, as General Ridgway has pointed out, an utter impossibility. As a matter of fact, only once in the entire advance did a ground patrol from X Corps make contact with a patrol from Eighth Army. There were not merely streams with no bridges. There were deep ravines, snow-clogged trails and towering mountains. The temperature at times dropped to 32 below zero. Almost 90 percent of the troops' energy, one officer declared, was expended in merely trying to keep warm. The troops had only leather boots, unfit for use in below-zero cold and snow, and they had no heavy overcoats. A story in *The New York Times* on November 15, 1950, tells something of what the troops were going through:

> ... The men have been cold night and day and now it appears that snow is arriving.
>
> The men of the First Cavalry have received most of their winter clothes but they still lack their heavy field overcoats and critically needed heavy "shoepacks," the Army's new Arctic boots and heavy socks to go with them.
>
> Doctors have started treating the first cases of trenchfoot, an affliction that was to have been made a thing of the past by the "shoepacks." ...

Other factors also are affecting the morale of the soldiers. Some of the line units have waited for as long as fourteen days for their cigarette issue.

This correspondent traveling up to the front saw cigarettes being issued at the Corps level in the morning.

The issue was free. In the evening he saw men smoking native tobacco rolled in toilet paper.

And later, when the weary, frozen soldiers at the front did get their cigarettes they had to pay for them—at the rate of 10 cents a package. . . .

General Ridgway also describes the misery as the 17th Regimental Combat Team of the 7th Division moved toward the Yalu:

None had insulated footwear and many had no gloves, while the clothing supply generally was short of winter-gear. . . . Food supplies were just barely sufficient . . .

At one point along the march a four man patrol volunteered to search out a crossing place for their battalion in a swift-running stream. Despite the merciless cold, the men waded into the nearly waist-deep river, and they were almost immediately encased in ice. They had to be put promptly into a warming tent and have their clothing cut off.

General Ridgway, who was following the progress of the advance from the Pentagon, confessed a sincere admiration for MacArthur's skills but was not blind to his faults. He assessed the advance on the Yalu in this manner in his book *The Korean War*:

While MacArthur's intense eagerness to complete his mission with dispatch is understandable, it is difficult to justify his plan and orders in the face of all that was known about the enemy's strength, his own supply situation, the terrain and the manner in which his own troops were dispersed— even had they been adequately equipped and at full strength, which was far from the case.

The 17th Regimental Combat team did indeed reach the Yalu, advancing against desultory Chinese resistance, and despite hunger, frostbite and the need, from time to time, to start their vehicles by pushing them. They had only summer oil for lubricant and that congealed quickly in the below-zero cold. But before they could even settle in on the frozen border, calamity overtook the Marine 1st Division at the Cho-sin Reservoir, far to the west and south.

General Smith had led his Marines most reluctantly up into this barren area, toward a group of huts that were his immediate objective. Convinced that he was being drawn into a trap, he had even complained to Rear Admiral Albert K. Morehouse on November 15, when the admiral was visiting Smith's command, about what he termed Almond's unrealistic planning and tendency to ignore enemy capabilities. He also wrote a letter to General Gates, the Marine Corps Commandant, repeating this complaint, insisting that Almond's orders were wrong and that he, Smith, did not intend to push his troops forward to destruction. But his protests were unavailing. Constantly prodded by Almond, he moved on, but took care to advance cohesively, stockpile gasoline and ammunition along the way, and maintain control of as much of the high ground as he could, above the main supply route. The whole division gave thanks that he did.

At the reservoir, the trap that Smith had feared and that MacArthur had ignored was finally sprung in a sudden explosion of firepower that, according to one Marine lieutenant who commanded a mortar platoon, looked like an old-fashioned Fourth of July, with Roman candles, rockets and sounding bugles, all bursting out of the bitter black night as if from another planet. With both flanks exposed, with no notion of the enemy's strength, and with inadequate weapons, the Marines fought the Chinese almost hand to hand, amazed sometimes at the size of this new enemy, compared to the relatively tiny Koreans. The battle went on day and night for some seventy-two hours. Marines learned never to zip up their sleeping bags when they sought rest, for Chinese would slip up at night and bayonet men who were still trying to free themselves to grab their guns. After a fight in the deep drifts, melted snow would run down into the mechanism of the BARs and freeze, so that in the next action the gun would not fire. Men with mild wounds—"million-dollar wounds" that ordinarily would mean a trip home—would freeze to death from being unable to move about.

The regulation .30-caliber carbine with which the Marines were armed was a low-velocity fairly primitive weapon. Some men cut them down into pistols. The M-1 rifle proved almost useless in night fighting. Yet the Marines took a fearsome toll of the Chinese, nearly decimating an entire Chinese army corps. Thanks largely to the skill of the Marine pilots, who, following directions from ground control, could lay their napalm with exquisite precision, the Marines hung to their positions and under General Smith's direction they completed an airstrip, with Chinese firing upon them from high ground. They blew holes in the ground to bury the truckloads of their frozen dead. Then they began their famous "attack to the rear" that enabled them to reach Hungnam in good order, bringing all their wounded, most of their equipment, and a contingent of Chinese prisoners.

Before this retreat was ordered there was an emergency secret meeting in Tokyo, of Generals Almond, Walker, Edwin K. Wright (G-3 in the Joint Strategic Plans and Operations Group), and Doyle Hickey (MacArthur's acting Chief of Staff), summoned by MacArthur to discuss the critical situation. General Almond, in his debriefing, recalled that "this conference confirmed General MacArthur's decision to readjust this front by withdrawing from contact with enemy until it was clearer to all concerned the extent of the invasion. . . . I immediately returned to my post in Korea. . . . There I directed the G-3 and the other staff officers to begin planning for the discontinuance of the X Corps attack to the northwest and the withdrawal of the Corps forces as a whole. . . ."

What General Almond failed to remember was that he insisted at this conference that, to quote General Wright, "conditions did not indicate the necessity for this action." General Wright also recalls that another point discussed at the meeting was the importance of placing Eighth Army and X Corps under one command. General Walker even offered to permit General Almond to take overall command instead of Walker. But Almond did not agree. MacArthur sent the commanders back to their posts and told them he would decide within a few days on both these matters. He did decide, of course, on the immediate withdrawal and he also ordered that, once X Corps had been safely returned to South Korea, it should come under Walker's command. But there was no talk of previous planning to pull these forces back.

Yet MacArthur in his *Reminiscences* declares that the withdrawal was part of the original plan, not only in the western sector but in the East, where Eighth Army had run into sudden massive Chinese resistance.

Actually, the withdrawal order for Eighth Army had been drawn up at Walker's own behest by Walker's Operations Officer General Dabney, as a contingency plan that was issued to the Corps commanders to be implemented when and if Walker's headquarters gave the word. Before he left for Tokyo, Walker authorized his Chief of Staff General Leven C. Allen to give that word when it became necessary. Allen sent out the order nine hours before Walker returned.

According to MacArthur, Eighth Army's withdrawal "was made with great skill." He regarded the professional part of the whole operation he said "with the greatest satisfaction." He felt, he proclaimed, long after the fact, that

> the hard decisions I had been forced to make, and the skill displayed by my field commanders had saved the army.... The movement north had upset the enemy's timetable, causing him to move prematurely, and to reveal the surreptitious massing of his armies. He hoped to quietly assemble a massive force until spring, and destroy us with one mighty blow. Had I not acted when I did we would have been a "sitting duck" doomed to eventual annihilation.

There is probably not an experienced battlefield commander alive who would dare present such a fantasy—of half a million soldiers bivouacked in the deep snows all winter long, awaiting the coming of spring, without giving a hint of their presence. To conceal and supply such a horde over a five-month period would require so much movement and such a concentration of men and equipment that air reconnaissance alone would have been enough to detect it. "Utterly fantastic!" said one famous leader upon reading this declaration.

MacArthur, in his *Reminiscences,* makes much of the fact that he had advised Washington of the heavy concentration of Chinese troops beyond the Yalu on November 3, reporting the presence of about half a million potential invaders. But if he had this information and knew, as of course he did, that there were no reinforcements available for his own force, why did he send his army plunging recklessly to the Yalu? Every able commander knows that enemy capabilities and not enemy intentions must be the measure by which he makes his plans.

General Walker, moving his forces across the Chongchon river toward the Yalu, had been given no hint of either enemy intentions or enemy capabilities. All he knew for sure was that there were Chinese out there *somewhere,* because Chinese soldiers, big men in long coats with white belts across their fronts as well as men in rubber shoes and quilted uniforms had already fired upon his troops and some had been captured. But all reports of their presence were belittled, or even pooh-poohed, as pure hallucination. To admit that the Chinese were there would be to say MacArthur was wrong. And there were very few hardy souls, even in the Pentagon, ready to utter such blasphemy.

The first hint of disaster to Eighth Army came when, as has been mentioned, the ROK II Corps on Walker's right flank, was sent into headlong flight by a massive Chinese assault. But before that there had been almost constant reports of large forces of Chinese in the area. Air and artillery bombardment had destroyed an enemy column southeast of Unsan, a village north of the Chongchon river where Eighth Army troops were positioned. A hundred horses and an uncounted number of Chinese soldiers had been left dead on the road. Elsewhere, air observers reported sighting moving columns of Chinese numbering in the thousands.

It was on November 1 that the ROK II Corps was eliminated as an effective fighting force. That evening, the 8th Cavalry Regiment experienced an attack by a large force of Chinese using mortars and rockets. With a wild blowing of bugles, playing notes that sounded like American Taps, a shrill of whistles, and shouted American obscenities, the Chinese materialized before these troops—troops who had been lulled into denying their existence, troops who had been dreaming already of the "homecoming" parade in Tokyo. And remember, it was November 3 when Mac-Arthur told the Joint Chiefs of Staff in the Pentagon of the massive buildup of forces across the Yalu.

On November 11, after the 8th Cavalry had lost more than half its strength in the battle at Unsan, General Walker wired MacArthur headquarters that he had been ambushed by "fresh, well-organized, and well-trained units, some of which were Chinese Communist forces." MacArthur's reply was a long time coming. When it came it was one more sharp reminder that Walker's forces were not moving ahead as rapidly as they had been scheduled to move.

Just two days before, MacArthur had told the Joint Chiefs in another gloomy message that the presence of large numbers of Chinese threatened "the ultimate destruction of the forces under my command." The Joint Chiefs then responded that the entrance of the Chinese into the war seemed an accomplished fact. But at this broad hint that the time might have come to think of halting his offensive, MacArthur sent cheery messages expressing full faith that his forces could destroy all armed resistance, while his air force could interdict all supply and reinforcement attempting to move across the Yalu, that complete victory was in reach and that it would be "fatal" to abandon this effort to bring hostilities to a glorious end. On November 24 he flew to Korea to give the signal for the

home-by-Christmas offensive. By this time turkeys had already been flown in to provide a Thanksgiving feast for the
front-line troops. And the railroad yards at Pyongyang
were filling up with cars bearing tons of Christmas goodies.
The "reconnaissance in force" was obviously closing both
eyes to what it had uncovered.

There was gloom and frustration at this time in the Pentagon. General Ridgway reports a long discussion in the
JCS War Room, where the Secretaries of War and Defense
both dwelt on the ominous outlook in Korea, "with no one
apparently willing to issue a direct order to the Far East
Commander to correct a state of affairs that was going rapidly from bad to worse." Finally, stung by his conscience,
Ridgway, having secured permission to speak, "blurted out
. . . that we had spent too much time on debate and that
immediate action was needed." He insisted, he recalls, that
"we owe it to the men in the field and to the God to whom
we must answer for those men's lives to stop talking and to
act." The reply to this outburst was utter silence, and the
meeting ended with no decision made. When Ridgway, in
the man-to-man discussion that followed, asked Hoyt
Vandenberg, Air Force chief, why the Chiefs did not send a
direct order and tell MacArthur what to do, Vandenberg
expressed out loud what the others must have felt. "What
good would that do? He wouldn't obey orders," are the
words Ridgway remembers. Of course, by this time it was
clear that MacArthur was disregarding their specific orders
to use no non-Korean troops in the provinces bordering the
Yalu. To this day Ridgway does not regret the response he
gave:

"You can relieve any commander who won't obey
orders, can't you?" The only reply to that challenge was a
look of puzzled amazement. Vandenberg walked away
without a word.

Ridgway was not the only one who ever observed that the Joint Chiefs seemed afraid of MacArthur. In May 1945, during World War II, General Joseph Stilwell observed to his diary that "Doug seemed out of control" and that the "War Department was afraid of him" (from D. Clayton James, *The Years of MacArthur*).

Whatever the reason, there was no calling MacArthur to account, nor did anyone remind him, as he continued to insist that he was engaged in "closing the vise" on the enemy, that his own intelligence officers now were telling of a buildup of Chinese forces in the reservoir area, where the Marines were headed, that "even now may be capable of . . . launching . . . a concerted drive to the south to cut off U.N. forces . . ."

By December 11, the Marine 1st Division, having fought its way out of the Chinese trap, had finally set itself up in the beachhead at Hungnam, ready to establish a defense perimeter and stay as long as need be, or to embark for the south and prepare to fight again. The Navy at this point performed one of the war's unsung miracles, equal to its accomplishment at Inchon. Without a single misstep, it moved out of Hungnam 105,000 troops, 17,000 vehicles, hundreds of thousands of tons of supplies, and 19,000 Korean refugees who had no zest for life among the Chinese Communists.

The Eighth Army too had begun its withdrawal on November 28, although many of its rear-area troops had taken off for safety well before that time, which was the date MacArthur issued his order for withdrawal.

MacArthur made this comment on the "retrograde movement":

Walker's skillful withdrawal was made with such speed that it led to many comments by ignorant correspondents that the troops were in flight. Nothing could have been further from the truth. The troops moved in good order and with unbroken cohesion among the various components. . . .

It was indeed true that the men who had done the fighting pulled back from the front lines in good order and, as they dropped farther and farther back into South Korea, even asked one another occasionally why they were not allowed to stop and hold against the enemy. But the actions of the rear-area troops, even the artillery, were often neither orderly nor good, although they were speedy.

One man who was much closer to the action than MacArthur or any of his court, described the withdrawal differently. General John H. Michaelis, who was then a colonel in command of the 27th Infantry Regiment, described in a letter his own observations:

> During the regiment's ordered retreat, we encountered scenes of panic that made me heartsick . . . What may not have been brought to your attention was the ever-present evidence of rout and cowardice of U.S. troops. My men could and were willing to stand and fight but no supplies were available and no logistical tail was available to support us. They had fled! Burning 8″ howitzers, carloads of 4.2″ mortar shells abandoned (always in extremely short supply). In Pyongyang we came across warehouses loaded with winter clothing, mail to ____Division, and in the rail yards carloads of ammo, gas, rations, etc. In particular one train of flatcars each loaded with the American tank with its secret fire control equipment—all abandoned and intact. We endeavored to destroy as much as possible by fire and by calling in air strikes but without too much success. The job was too immense.
>
> The orderly withdrawal of front line troops belies the haste and panic of those behind the front to "bug out." Witness Army Headquarters in Taegu and later planned moves to Pusan when we were still in Pyongyang (as I recall). [Letter dated June 13, 1978.]

Other eyewitness accounts agree with that of General Michaelis. One private first class of the 118th Battalion of Combat Engineers, recalls the vain efforts to destroy the secret tank equipment, after rear-area officers had abandoned it, having decided they lacked authority to have it demolished. He remembers too the grumbling among the troops when they had to abandon well-dug-in positions they felt sure they could have held, to follow the bug-out brigade southward. The artillery, he recalls, desperate to use up their ammunition, kept calling for "targets! targets!" firing at maximum range, with guns so worn that shells were "keyholing" as they passed over the heads of the infantry.

Colonel John Austin, Secretary of I Corps General Staff, in a long talk, described the panic and confusion he found in the rear area as the bug-out fever spread, with wild rumors afloat that this unit or that unit to left or right had already taken flight. Officers and troops fought each other for room on jeeps and trucks. At Kunu-ri, Austin saw no sign of the enemy. But "friendlies," he said, were running in all directions. Good-sized units disintegrated before his eyes as they scrambled to find wheels, pulling their officers out of vehicles to make room for themselves, and shouting that the Chinese were coming by the thousands and that "we'll all be surrrounded!" Night was coming on and the Chinese did much of their fighting at night. And rumors magnified. A platoon "in trouble" on the front line would become "Front caving in!" at Corps level. Our artillery, according to Austin, had run off and abandoned almost all their self-propelled weapons, and trainloads of military hardware. The advancing Chinese soon began to make use of the cast-off guns and ammunition, pouring 75-mm. and 105-mm. shells upon the retreating troops in unheard-of quantities, as many as 7,000 rounds in one night. But there was no close pursuit. The Chinese had obviously not expected the sudden wholesale withdrawal and were not equipped for sustained action. Their front-line troops had no specific objectives. Men just fought their way forward until their rice gave out. Then they fell back for new supplies.

The retreating units, meanwhile, took to the southbound road with every vehicle they could find—weapons-carriers, trucks, tractors, tanks. No plans had been made (despite MacArthur's story) for phased withdrawal. No points had been selected where the troops might rally and regroup. They were just headed south. (And Army headquarters, as Michaelis pointed out in his letter, was now far, far behind the front—at Taegu, where it had been situated during the fighting on the Pusan perimeter.)

Fortunately, the Chinese never committed any major elements of their air force. Soldiers on the retreat recall only "bed check Charlie," a sputtering plane that sounded "like a Piper with a badly synchronized engine," from which an armed mortar round would be dropped by hand just as darkness fell. Indeed, according to front-line reports, sometimes only one in five of the attacking Chinese would be armed. They counted on picking up weapons on the field. And some carried only spears fashioned out of sharpened lengths of automobile spring fastened to poles. They moved mostly on foot, although officers sometimes led them on horseback. And they attacked at night, taking full advantage of the fact that the American troops had no experience at night fighting and were prone to yield ground when they found the enemy slipped by them in the dark.

Too often panic among rear-area troops was triggered by sudden disappearance of the officer and staff, who left the

GIs to work out their own salvation. It was a repetition in
many ways of the scenes described by Marguerite Higgins
during the earlier retreat from Seoul. She wrote then of
one sergeant who said of the vanishing officers: "Those
sons of bitches are trying to save their own hides . . . there
are planes coming but the brass won't talk. They're afraid
there might not be room for everybody."

There were no planes coming to rescue the men engaged
near Kunu-ri. But when colleagues went in search of the
Commander of IX Corps, General John Coulter (known to
junior officers as "John the Nervous"), they could not find
him. He had apparently left the field on some errand. (He
was relieved of his post when General Ridgway took over
command of the Eighth Army soon afterward.)

But other officers who were leading their troops in battle, ready to hang on despite the bug-out behind them,
performed deeds of courage and ingenuity that saved hundreds of lives—and brought neither medals nor accolades.

The 17th Regimental Combat Team of the 7th Division,
operating at the peacetime level of 85 percent of its
strength, was the only United States unit actually to reach
the banks of the Yalu. Their withdrawal from that dangerous position, after the sudden Chinese offensive took
shape, was another small miracle of determination, skill,
courage and resourcefulness. Under command of Colonel
H. B. Powell, the regiment, moving by night and day over
rugged, unmapped terrain, withdrew from the high ground
swiftly and in good order. They found and made good use
of a narrow-gauge railroad to speed their descent and employed ore-buckets on an overhead line, at an abandoned
Japanese mining operation to carry their heavy equipment
across a wide gap in the mountains where there were no
roads at all.

Even more notable was the manner in which General (then Colonel) Paul L. Freeman, Jr., extricated his 23rd Regimental Combat Team from what he termed a "suicidal position" near Kunu-ri, just below the Chungchon river some seventy miles from the Yalu. General Freeman, in an interview with Colonel James Ellis in April 1974, still confessed himself bewildered by the reasoning behind General MacArthur's ordering the general advance in November 1950.

> The night before the attack began [he said] Colonel Claire E. Hutchin, Jr., and I had dinner with our division commander, Brigadier General Lawrence D. Keiser, and we expressed ... our inability to understand what was going on and we could only conclude that General MacArthur had some very, very secret information that these Chinese were not really going to resist. ...

The Chinese, of course, not only resisted but turned the attack back on itself with massive forces. The 24th Infantry Regiment, according to General Freeman, were "straggled, lost, defeated, and disorganized." His own regiment was designated as the rear guard for IX Corps, to hold fast until all the divisions had cleared. His 1st Battalion under Colonel Hutchin, deployed at least three times, "held off all the Chinese and never lost a man, until all of the divisions had passed south of Kunu-ri." Yet the IX Corps in general, Freeman recalled, seemed to exercise no control or direction during the entire battle. He did not know until much later that the commanding general of the Corps, John Coulter (who liked to be called by his middle name, Breitling) had departed the field before the battle was well joined.

When Freeman's regiment drew back to Kunu-ri, he said, "all was in confusion. The Turks (the Turkish Brigade attached to IX Corps) had been committed but they had taken one look at the situation and they had no stomach for it and they were running in all directions."

Colonel John Michaelis, on Freeman's left, where his Wolfhound Regiment acted as rear guard for I Corps, received personal instructions from his Corps commander, General Milburn, to move out, west, down the road to Anju. But Freeman had received no instructions except to hold a defensive position near Kunu-ri, until the 2nd Division had cleared. And the division had run into a roadblock, without the strength to break through. "The division," Freeman related, "was running the gauntlet and most of them were running for their lives and not making much progress." And because the troops still in front of the 23rd Regimental Combat Team were scattered over the area, it was impossible for Freeman to bring artillery fire on the enemy to help them out.

At about this time, Freeman turned to his executive officer, Colonel Frank Meszar, and told him, "Well, this is it!" Together they laid out all the arms and ammunition in their possession and decided that here was the place where they were going to stand and die. But Freeman also told Meszar (and this may be contrasted with MacArthur's observation, from eight hundred miles away, that the troops moved "in good order with unbroken cohesion"), "You are seeing a sight few have ever seen—an entire U.S. Army Corps in rout and flight, abandoning their equipment and wounded."

Division communications had broken down, but Freeman was able to reach the Assistant Division Commander General Joseph S. Bradley, at 9th Regiment headquarters,

to report conditions from Freeman's point of view. Freeman urgently recommended to the general that his regiment be ordered to move out before dark, lest it and the
other units be demolished there. A message from an airplane, dropped by the artillery commander of IX Corps,
confirmed Freeman's own assessment of the outlook. But
Division Commander General Keiser apparently had
nothing to go on but an order prohibiting a move to Anju.
And of course, by this time the Corps commander was long
gone to some place where he could not be found. Finally,
just before dark, General Bradley took it on himself to
order the withdrawal to Anju, and Freeman, the remnants
of the scattered 24th Regiment having finally been cleared,
made ready to move west. To clear his way, he fired his
entire remaining basic artillery load, burning out the tubes
of all his howitzers. Except for that, his unit would never
have got through. As it was, they came out almost intact,
except for their artillery, bringing vehicles and all equipment, having suffered only a few combat losses. Of all the
units in that division, only Freeman's emerged "intact and
combat worthy." "But we couldn't have held off the entire
Chinese Army from our position there at Kunu-ri," Freeman said.

In commenting on the attack and its consequences, General Freeman in a letter sent long afterward declared, "The
initial defeat of the US troops by the Chinese intervention
in November 1950 was MacArthur's fault and not theirs. The
resulting withdrawal I can assure you was not planned—
and why should anyone share such a ridiculous idea?"

Only MacArthur could answer that.

What really brought an end to the bug-out fever was a
tragic accident that forced a change in command in
Korea—a change that altered the whole character of the

war, of the army, of the leadership. And the accident was caused, as most modern accidents are, by reckless speed.

General Walton Walker, called "Johnny" and code-named "Scotch Six", had just finished assuring the men of I Corps as he sat in his jeep at Suwon that he was "not going to permit the flanks of this magnificent army to be turned" and that he would see it all "safely withdrawn from Korea." He then sped on to offer the same message to IX Corps. With his shiny Patton-style helmet and his hell-for-leather air he sent his jeep at breakneck speed through village and countryside, scattering natives and livestock. In a village north of Seoul, Walker's jeep ran almost head-on into a pickup driven by a Korean. The truck hooked the jeep's rear fender and sent it into a flip. Walker was thrown from his seat and died almost instantly. (Scuttlebutt among soldiers who had been near the scene was that the driver of the pickup was promptly executed by a Korean policeman.) Walker's promise of safe withdrawal never reached IX Corps.

MacArthur soon after the retreat began informed Washington that his current plans provided for "a withdrawal in successive positions to the Pusan area." And his Corps and Division commanders were soon employed in working out the details of such a withdrawal and, along with the troops, were dreaming of the sound of the transport whistles that would carry them back home.

Life, at least at Corps level, had cooled down to a pleasant routine, with liquor aplenty, time aplenty for gin rummy games, and no disturbing intelligence from any source. There was no contact with the enemy, and no one, according to one staff officer, wanted any. There were no patrols, no armored reconnaissance, and very little communication from one Corps to another, there being few relays on the mountaintops to carry radio messages. Some messages were sent via Tokyo.

At about this time, an unsigned article appeared in the California magazine *Fortnight,* concerning conditions at the Almond headquarters in Hungnam. *Time* later identified the author as Otto Sporrer, chaplain of the 1st Marines. Here is part of what he said:

> [At] X Corps headquarters, the Officers' Mess consisted of a nice warmed building in which food was served in plates, well cooked. There were waiters and an orchestra available for music. Outside in the bitter cold, long lines of enlisted men stood in order to receive a little heated can of C rations. Those long lines took three hours to feed.

According to John Austin, secretary to the I Corps general staff, there was only one attempt at I Corps to learn where the enemy could be and what he might be up to. General Milburn, in December, asked Austin to accompany him, in an unarmed L-5 plane with a fiberglass canopy, over enemy territory. They flew around for three hours, as far as twenty miles north of where the Chinese lines were supposed to be, and sometimes as low as one hundred feet over the snow, and found no sign. The Chinese, they knew, often wore white coveralls over their uniforms when encamped in snow country and were adept at sitting motionless for hours. The two searchers found never a track.

But the enemy was there, already looking for gaps in the line, of which there were plenty, particularly between I and IX Corps, and he was undoubtedly already at work on preparations for the New Year's offensive that would force the United Nations forces back across the Han. Rumors were still current of the approach of "Chinese hordes."

("How many Chinese in a horde?" some disrespectful GIs used to ask one another.) And there were the usual fairy tales of the disintegration of some unit or other beyond the horizon. A joke that quickly grew tiresome among the junior officers was this:

"Have you heard that the 24th Division has been relieved?"

"By whom? The British Commonwealth Division?"

"No. By the Chinese!"

But the joking stopped when General Walker's replacement arrived, on the wings of a bitter December breeze, after just barely avoiding a fatal slam into the side of a mountain that the pilot did not see until after he had touched down at the Taegu airport. Some officers, on first meeting General Ridgway, snickered at the hand grenades (live ones, he asserted) that he wore on his shoulder harness. Some GIs were outraged when he ordered all the cute slogans and pictures removed from Army vehicles, and the machines to be repainted straight GI. But the field commanders were very quickly snapped out of their torpor by his new regime.

Ridgway's first job was to make some effort to stem the impending Chinese offensive. MacArthur had given him only one specific directive—to maintain his forces as far in advance as possible and to hold on to Seoul unless there was danger that it would become a citadel position. By this time MacArthur had grown suddenly knowledgeable about the Chinese, whose very presence he was, just a few weeks ago, so earnestly denying. He warned Ridgway that the Chinese were far stronger than they seemed, that they did not rely on the roads or on daylight to advance but came in at night over hills and ridges. (In his first assessment, when he had promised to exterminate them, MacArthur had apparently expected the Chinese to advance by means of highway and railroad through Sinuiju where they would have been prime targets for our Air Force.) And he noted too that the Chinese infantry depended more extensively on its own firepower than ours did.

"The entire Chinese military establishment is in this fight," he declared. He told Ridgway he had been urging the Joint Chiefs to order an attack by land, sea and air on the Chinese mainland (a move that would have one immediate effect—it would have turned the fight into a global encounter, for which some of our allies had no taste at all). And strangely, considering his later "campaign" statements to the effect that failure to permit him the use of the Air Force to cut off supplies from Manchuria had made victory impossible. MacArthur also told Ridgway that air power could not isolate the battlefield and could not halt the flow of troops and supplies.

Ridgway writes of his own dismay on New Year's morning to meet, on the road north of Seoul, truckloads of ROK soldiers who had thrown away their pistols and rifles, fleeing in utter disorder southward, followed by straggling ranks of soldiers on foot who had no aim but to get as far away as possible from the attacking Chinese. Unable to find anyone who could speak English, Ridgway could only stand and wave his arms in vain, while trucks and foot soldiers dodged around him. Finally he stopped one truck containing Korean officers who knew English. They listened to him, but they did not obey; soon the whole disorderly parade was streaming past once more.

A battalion of United States infantry had been caught up in the retreat, and Ridgway, visiting their wounded next day, found them, he said, "thoroughly dispirited." But he did manage to halt the retreat at last by setting up strag-

gler posts far in the rear where American MPs halted the
runaways and helped reorganize and rearm them. With his
first task completed, Ridgway sized up his situation. The
headlong flight of the ROKs had left his right flank wide
open. Thousands of panic-stricken refugees threatened to
overwhelm the bridges over the half-frozen Han. There
were a hundred thousand U.N. troops to bring across the
river, along with all their heavy equipment, including British Centurion tanks and American 8-inch howitzers, and
they would need all the bridge room available. Ridgway
thereupon decided to begin the withdrawal at once. He
sent word to the Rhee government and staff to hie themselves out of Seoul to safety by 3 P.M. After that he used his
MPs to restrain all civilian traffic while the troops and
equipment crossed. Ridgway came along then in his jeep,
with the weary, shivering parade of refugees close behind
him in the dusk.

Ridgway wrote afterward, "When the big 8-inch howitzers and the Centurion tanks came along my heart rose
into my throat and remained there while the bridge sagged
deep in the rushing water. A combat-loaded Centurion
tank, I knew, exceeded the rated tonnage capacity of the
bridge."

But the Army and the equipment and the refugees all
crossed in safety, and the Army soon took up strong defensive positions south of the river, that they were never again
to yield.

Ridgway began immediately to examine the possibilities
of getting back across the river in sufficient strength to do
damage to the enemy. He had asked the Eighth Army
staff, mostly inherited from General Walker, to prepare for
him a staff study on "desirable location of major elements
of the Eighth Army for the period February 20 to August

31, 1951." They handed Ridgway's G-3, General F. W.
Moorman, a fat volume that described a phased withdrawal to the Pusan area by April 15 (in accordance with
the MacArthur scenario) with embarkation (Oh, word with
every comfort fraught!) on April 16. Moorman would not
even read it, and he warned the staff that Ridgway would
never approve. Ridgway too spared it no more than a
glance before he marked it, in his vigorous angular hand,
"Disapproved." He handed it back to Moorman, but
Moorman insisted he keep it himself. Twenty-five years
later, it was still in Ridgway's possession.

But considering MacArthur's own plan, Ridgway did
have to cope with the possibility that the Army would have
to be withdrawn from Korea in good order. So he set Brigadier General Garrison Davidson to work preparing the
"Davidson Line" far to the south around the Pusan area,
with sandbags, trenches, artillery emplacements, even
barbed wire. The bags and barbed wire at least proved
useful to the Korean laborers who worked on the project,
for they and their neighbors eventually made off with most
of the material, once it became clear the Army was not
going to find refuge there. For Ridgway was thinking in
terms of attack and was concerned immediately with shaking the last traces of bug-out fever from the hearts of the
unit commanders.

He gathered General Milburn of I Corps, General
Coulter of IX Corps (X Corps was still being reorganized in
the Pusan area after the retreat from Hungnam) and Colonel William A. Collier, Eighth Army Deputy Chief of Staff,
together in the brick schoolhouse at Suwon that served as
headquarters, to decide with them what needed to be done
to return the troops to fighting trim. They talked of many
things, but specifically of mines and searchlights and com-

munications; then Ridgway laid before them his plan for an eventual recrossing of the Han to establish a two-division beachhead on the north bank, a limited-objective attack, shallow in nature, small in scope, on a reduced front—but the first move in a major advance he would name "Operation Killer."

"The period of reaction is over," Ridgway told the officers. "We are going to attack. By the first of March we are going to close on the south bank of the Han!"

After Ridgway had left the room, the three officers looked at one another with what may or may not have been a wild surmise. One said: "He's crazy!" Another said: "Impossible!" Only Milburn could see that "it might be done."

Ridgway then undertook a survey of the Army's fighting potential and learned to his dismay that the troops were far from ready, with much of the leadership sharing the general distaste for thought of further combat. He listened to gripes, checked into shortages and began to sort out the leaders that had no heart for the job. An ordnance officer who did not know what he had in his depots ("I can only forward the reports I get," he averred) was sent back to Japan to take over some less demanding chore. Another officer, who "did not know what was wrong" that prevented the mail from reaching the troops on time and who explained "I can't be everywhere at once," was assured that he was not going to be everywhere, that he was going to be riding the mail truck until the trouble was located and mended. And all the infantry unit commanders were told to get off the roads and into the hills, to go back to the days of their service forebears if need be and use smoke signals and runners if radio contact could not be maintained.

An officer who dared to assure Ridgway that it was "impossible" to get hot food up to the front lines was immediately fired. And the troops were quickly provided with at least one hot meal every day from rolling kitchens. Helicopters were called on to bring the stationery to the troops, who had been bitching about its lack. The sight of soldiers without gloves prompted Ridgway to order an immediate shipment of extra gloves to all the combat units.

The sudden rolling of lopped-off heads to left and right awakened many an officer to the fact that more things were possible than he had ever imagined. And the sight of the Army commander on the battlefield lifted the hearts of many dispirited GIs.

Ridgway canceled a "hold at all costs" order and ruled that no such order should ever be given unless he had himself assessed the specific situation. The forward command post of Eighth Army was moved out of the comfort of the city where it was located and placed up close to the front, near the center of the line, in two tents heated with a small stove and furnished with cot, table and chair. Here General Ridgway felt he was just as comfortable as he needed to be, right on the edge of the dry bed of the Han river, with an airstrip newly bulldozed out close by so he could get aloft and look over the terrain and the action whenever it suited him, or fly to Tokyo to confer with the C in C.

By mid-January General Ridgway felt he had sufficiently revived the fighting spirit and sharpened the efficiency of Eighth Army to start pushing forward again to discover where the enemy was lodged. Scouting flights with Air Force General Earle Partridge in an old A-T training plane had revealed no signs; still, he had not come to Korea merely to find a warm spot to wait in, and it was not his plan to crawl back to button up his troops in the Pusan perimeter, from which they had broken free with

the Inchon invasion. So he began his advance on January
25, with the aim of establishing I Corps and IX Corps on
the south bank of the Han, whence the two-division crossing might be launched to establish the desired bridgehead
on the other side. While more than one or two unit commanders were still loath to abandon their comfortable garrison life, most of them took welcome pride in the sight of
the refreshed Army moving forward in two mighty columns, loaded with terrifying fire power, under unified
command and tight control, knowing exactly what their
mission was.

There was brutal and bloody fighting in the next weeks
and a sudden retreat by the 2nd Division, when the collapse of an ROK Division, fleeing in panic again from a
Chinese night attack, left the 2nd Division flank exposed.
Colonel Paul Freeman's 23rd Regimental Combat Team
had to stage another grim defense to hold off a superior
force of Chinese, this time at Chipyong-ni, near the rail
center of Wonju.

Freeman's force this time consisted of only two battalions—his own 3rd Battalion and a French battalion commanded by a lieutenant colonel who, using the *nom de
guerre* of "Ralph Monclar," had accepted a reduction in
rank from lieutenant general just so he might lead this
small portion of the United Nations forces in battle. Monclar had a bad leg, a reminder of one of the thirteen
wounds he had received in World War I; still he insisted
on leading his force in person. As a result his battalion
moved so slowly that they reached their destination with
barely daylight enough left to set up their defense—a difficult job when they lacked the force to establish a perimeter
sufficiently large to contain their artillery and had to position them in a separate zone with but one rifle company for
security. And Colonel Freeman was embarrassed very

early by having to scold his French "general" for lighting
bonfires that gave away the position of his forces.

The fight began soon after midnight and lasted all night
and all day with fighting seesawing on and off the nearby
ridges, which had to be retaken several times by bayonet
charges. This time too, as at Kunu-ri, Colonel Freeman
faced what he felt was his final stand. Low winter clouds
had reduced visibility to near zero, and it was impossible
for the embattled troops to receive air support. With the
surrounding Chinese attacking in division strength, the
end seemed very near. Just before night fell, however, the
skies cleared and the Marine pilots flew in to provide close
support. This ended the Chinese attack; they fled the field,
leaving uncounted dead. At dawn, the survivors looked out
on a gruesome sight—hundreds upon hundreds of Chinese
corpses, frozen stiff in their padded-cotton uniforms, many
without a sign of a wound.

Only a few days after this battle, MacArthur arrived at
Wonju, where the X Corps tactical command post was located, and where Ridgway showed him an "eyes only"
memorandum outlining Ridgway's plans for Operation
Killer, that was to be sent that day to all Corps commanders, and to the ROK Chief of Staff. Attending this conference were, besides MacArthur and Ridgway, Lieutenant
General Almond (he had been promoted just five days earlier), Major General Courtney Whitney, Major General
Doyle Hickey, of MacArthur's staff, and Lieutenant Colonel Tony Story, MacArthur's aide and pilot. MacArthur
approved Ridgway's plan and soon afterward called a news
conference, which was attended by correspondents from
major United States newspapers and news services. With
Ridgway leaning on a table in the back of the room, Mac-
Arthur quietly announced:

"I have just ordered a resumption of the offensive."

The calm remark went through Ridgway like a hot stick. MacArthur had ordered nothing of the sort. Ridgway had ordered it, and MacArthur had merely approved. As a good soldier, Ridgway of course held his peace, although his stomach must have been churning. Shortly afterward, he heard the voice of the Commander in Chief on the radio, telling the world: "I have just ordered the Eighth Army to resume the offensive." Ridgway turned to his staff:

"Does anyone have a copy of that order?" he demanded. "Has anyone *seen* it?" No one had.

In Ridgway's own copy of MacArthur's *Reminiscences,* he has printed carefully in pen and ink, beside and beneath the sentence *I ordered Ridgway to start north again,* "No such order was ever issued."

(A significant instance of the degree to which General Almond would hasten to support his Commander in Chief, even in his falsehoods, is an entry in Almond's diary, an obvious "posterity paper," as Dean Acheson would have termed it:

> 20 Feb 10:30 Arrival of CINC UNC [MacArthur], Maj Gen Hickey, Acting C/S CHQ, FEC: Maj Gen Courtney Whitney, Lt. Col Story, Aide and Pilot to CINC. Conference at WONJU. Operation "Killer" was described to CINC, who approved.
> 11:00 Ridgway joined conference.

Who would dream from reading that innocent entry that Ridgway brought the plan for Operation Killer along with him, in "eyes only" form, just as he had written it, and that the CINC could not possibly have read it until after Ridgway got there?)

Indeed, just after the Chinese New Year's offensive had

retaken Seoul and driven the U.N. forces back across the Han, MacArthur had advised the Joint Chiefs of Staff that, if he was to receive no more reinforcements, and Chiang was not to be "unleashed" (which would have been rather like unleashing a superannuated and toothless watchdog), and there was to be no attack on mainland China, then, unless there were overriding political considerations, "the command should be withdrawn from Korea just as soon as it is tactically possible to do so."

Yet, in his *Reminiscences,* this line appears:

". . . the thought of defeat in Korea had never been entertained by me."

4

plots and counterplots

It has long been Communist gospel that the Korean War was begun by South Korean forces, instigated by the United States, in furtherance of a plot among MacArthur, Truman, Rhee and Chiang Kai-shek to involve the United States in a war they hoped would wipe out Communism in China and possibly even in the rest of the world. And there were instances enough of Rhee's intent to lead his forces into North Korea so that this theory seemed to hold some substance. South Korean armed units made frequent forays into North Korean territory in the years before the outbreak, probably as often as the North Korean forces staged raids of their own across the 38th parallel. Certainly hostilities bristled there frequently enough to convince many observers that open war was inevitable.

But the notion that the war was begun by an organized invasion on the part of the South Korean Constabulary, which had no more armor than a few scout cars and half-tracks, no air force at all, no antitank guns, and fewer than a hundred howitzers of limited range, is too fantastic for a reasonable person to entertain. Of course Syngman Rhee had been threatening such an attack since the day he took power and seemed to have built up in his own mind a picture of a rejoicing army of patriots (himself at the head) who would rally the entire countryside about them as they marched north to drive the Reds back into the wild wastes of Manchuria. But the United States authorities, made uneasy by these boasts, had taken care to withhold from Rhee the arms and supplies that would have made such an excursion even worth thinking about.

North Korea on the other hand, where the Communists had the advantage of owning a large force of battle-hardened veterans of the fight against the Japanese in China, had been well armed by the Russians, who left behind them, when they pulled out their occupying force, tons of used, slightly outdated, but far-from-obsolete equipment, and sent in, just before the war broke out, heavy artillery, T-34 tanks, automatic weapons and brand-new planes to the number of more than 150.

The major advantage of the North Koreans, however, lay in training and morale. They had leaders who had been seasoned in the Chinese Eighth Route Army or had served in the Red Army in World War II, and each division had about fifteen Russian army advisers. The ROK Constabulary, on the other hand, was too often led, as has already been observed, by self-seeking native politicos who had neither training nor taste for battle, plus a number of Japanese-trained veterans whom most Koreans looked on as traitors. And American Army advisers were frequently overruled or ignored by Korean superiors, who were more jealous of the prerogatives of their rank than they were eager for schooling in modern warfare.

To engage in an invasion of the size with which the war began required weeks of planning and staging, of moving troops and equipment into position, of plotting artillery concentrations so as to bring major targets under immediate fire. To sugget that the invasion was the impromptu response to an attack by the ill-prepared ROK Constabulary is ridiculous.

Equally ridiculous was the fairy tale endorsed by the extreme right wing, fostered to a slight extent by MacArthur, and earnestly promoted by Syngman Rhee and his most wild-eyed followers. This was the legend that the war was begun as a first step toward world conquest by the Moscow-centered Communist conspiracy, a conspiracy that may have included Dean Acheson, United States Secretary of State, many of his advisers and underlings, some shadowy White House figures, probably a few faceless traitors in the Pentagon, spies in the foreign services of both United States and England, plus a few pro-Communists in the American occupation forces.

To accept this scenario, one had to believe that the North Koreans were mere pawns of the Chief Conspirator, Joseph Stalin, ready to fling themselves blindly into battle whenever he gave the word—and all secretly yearning to be freed from his yoke, to find safety in the arms of Syngman Rhee. One also had to believe for instance that the North Korean soldiers went into battle only under compulsion, to escape certain death or some even more dreadful fate, holding their places in line only as long as their bonds restrained them. And this is exactly how Syngman Rhee described their lot, in letters he sent to MacArthur. Here for instance are paragraphs from one dated August 12, 1950:

... the enemy seems capable of drawing on unlimited man-power resources. Their recruiting system is so ruthless that they have forced small school boys to fight.

Many school children are ordered into the Communist frontline at gunpoint with only a few days gun practice. Another serious aspect of this problem is the apparent fact that the enemy is able to draw on an almost unlimited supply of arms and ammunition. This coupled with their tactics of forcing whole town populations to fight for them poses a grave problem. In some places for example young school boys, some 13 and 14 years old, march to the front while Russian or North Korean officers keep them at gunpoint. Another example is the fact we have found the drivers of Russian-made tanks wired to their seats so that they will fight to the death.

It is doubtful that MacArthur accepted these horror stories seriously, although he did take pains to keep the old man mollified without actually yielding to any of his requests for more and more arms.

Still, MacArthur certainly would have agreed that the North Korean People's Army was no more than a sort of advance guard in Joe Stalin's march toward world conquest. He must have known, however, as all his field commanders soon learned, that the NKPA was highly motivated, a band of fierce, even vicious warriors who acted as if they were in a fight to the death, as indeed many of them were, while the ROK, or South Korean army, in the beginning showed very little zeal for battle.

It was a strange fact, probably never noted by Mac-Arthur, that the two armies—NKPA and ROK—had the identical war aim, the unification of their country. The front ranks of the NKPA were filled with men who had devoted most of their lives to fighting the Japanese oppression and were now taking up the Communist banner only because it seemed to be leading them in the best and last shot at unifying their homeland under native rule. The ROK army, once the political pets had been shaken out of the leadership, never equaled in fanatic determination the NKPA troops that led the first invasion, but they soon learned to fight with true ferocity in the hope of putting their country together again.

There was nothing in the Korean nature that bred either cowardice or distaste for physical combat. Indeed, the Koreans, when aroused, would fight like cornered cats and could play as rough as the Americans or the Chinese. United States Marines were once astounded at the ferocity with which Korean troops would engage in the game of "chicken fighting," in which one man would sit on another's shoulders to go battle an opponent similarly mounted. The two would belabor each other until teeth came loose, eyes closed and blood ran free—all in the name of sport. And when a sham battle was staged as part of the training program of ROK units, one group, frustrated when their "ammunition" took no visible effect, picked up stones and began to hurl them with full force at the "enemy."

The ordinary stay-at-home Korean who had been neither a "collaborator"—as almost any person who attained any status at all in Korea was bound to be under the Japanese rule—nor a "Communist"—which was the name for all who dared take up a strong stand against Syngman Rhee—actually seemed to care little which side might "win" the war, as long as the country was united. When the NKPA swept everything before it on the way to take over the whole peninsula, many of the plain people openly or privately cheered them on. And when MacArthur in his turn looked as if he might put the country together under one rule, they made him a hero too. They even began to believe that he might be the reincarnation of the famous Chinese military leader, Kwan Yu, who lived in folklore as the savior of the Land of Morning Calm.

There was, none the less, a long-time, although mild, hostility between North Korea and South Korea, a hang-over from the ancient days when the Three Kingdoms had divided up the nation North and South. The hostility was no stronger than the mild contempt Southerners in our land hold for Yankees, and that Yankees often reciprocate with equal fervor. The North Korean, to the well-brought-up folk in the South, was a boor, a roughneck, unlettered and unable even to speak his native tongue without growl-ing. And to the North Korean the South Korean was a lily-fingered softy, afraid to dirty his hands with labor and given to all sorts of petty, effeminate vices. Every province in Korea long had its own accent. But the Northern accent was instantly recognizable, so that once the war began it was not always safe for a North Korean in a Southern city even to open his mouth.

But as the tide of the war ebbed and flowed, there were men and women in every village who changed coats as rap-idly as the village changed hands. And maps erected in public to mark the progress of the MacArthur armies were used with equal devotion to indicate the advances of the armies of Kim Il Sung.

Some Western journalists seized on the very name of the North Korean premier, Kim Il Sung, as evidence of a dark conspiracy of sorts. For Kim Il Sung was the name of a Ko-rean hero of long ago and merely a *nom de guerre* for the current premier, a fellow obviously too young to have per-formed the legendary deeds. There were, however, perhaps as many Korean fighting men who had adopted the name

Kim Il Sung as there were American boxers, when the century was new, who called themselves Kid McCoy. Just which Kim was the real McCoy no one any longer could say. Nor did anyone much care. Almost every North Korean citizen knew that Kim Il Sung was really Kim Sung Chu.

Although there were no high-level conspiracies to set the Koreans at each other's throats, there were, both North and South, a number of leading figures who were prompted by motives they never would have owned up to in public. The political situation in the North was not simply a matter of hiding the Soviet face behind the façade of a group of native puppets who would act only when Joe Stalin moved his fingers. It was necessary to win the minds of the plain Koreans and to earn their devotion. This cause was nearly lost at the start by the behavior of the occupying Soviet troops who first entered North Korea. They were by no means the elite of the Red Army and had been engaged for many months in merely immobilizing a share of the Japanese strength by holding positions opposite the Japanese forces in Manchuria. When they were finally turned loose on the Japanese, a few days before the first atom bomb was dropped on Japan, they chased them through North Korea, killing all they could reach, then turned on the native population, raping, robbing, brutalizing in the manner of undisciplined and action-hungry troops in every war.

But they were soon brought to heel by the commissars, who taught them the necessity of winning the hearts of the peasantry. And the native Communists who returned after service with the Red Armies were greeted as heroes. The Russians promptly accepted the People's Committees as the government in being, and the People's Committees program of expropriation of Japanese property was soon put into effect, to the delight of the populace, most of whom had been tenant farmers or had been engaged in "fire field" farming—burning off woodland to provide farm plots which they could cultivate until the authorities caught up with them. Under the direction of the Russians and later the North Korean government that took over with Russian blessing (and oversight), Japanese land and factories were turned over to the people who worked them—provided they evinced loyalty to the Communist regime.

But the North Korean politicians werre not without ambitions of their own. The most militant of the current crop was probably Pak Yon Hong, a member of the Communist Party who had fled South Korea to escape Rhee's purge. He appeared to be the logical man to lead the North Korean Communist government, except that Kim Il Sung seemed ready to outdo him in militance. Many Koreans still believe that the decision to invade the South was an effort on the part of Kim Il Sung to steal much of Pak Yon Hong's thunder. While the decision surely had the approval of Moscow, it was still one that was made in Pyongyang.

MacArthur's motives were not nearly so easy to read, but he was surely prompted by something beyond military necessity or the call of duty, when he disregarded directives and risked the wholesale destruction of so much of his army. It is even possible, by reading the record and assigning selfish motives where no other seems to fit, to trace through MacArthur's career a pattern of deep concern with his own private ambitions, petty interests and public image that overrode considerations of military advantage, duty, and even common sense. In World War II, there was his apparent attempt to dissociate himself from the Bataan disaster, as well as his strange refusal to talk to General

Brereton, when the Japanese upset the MacArthur scenario by attacking the Philippines; his diligent effort to
make it appear that his communiqués (from 500 miles behind the lines) came from the front; the exaggerations and
falsehoods concerning dates of victory and enemy losses;
his willingness to accept public credit for the accomplishments of General Eichelberger; his use of troops to further
private political ends in the southern Philippines when
they were badly needed in Luzon; his hanging on to naval
units needed elsewhere, until the matter of supreme command was decided in his favor; his reckless plans to "con-
quer" Java with hopelessly inadequate forces; his ban on
air bombing of Manila ("to spare the civilians") while allowing artillery shelling of the city which was every bit as
damaging to the civilians but less likely to wreck his own
lavish apartment atop a Manila hotel. Before that there
was his selection of the title "Field Marshal" for his job at
the head of the ragtag Philippine army, plus his designing
of a childishly ornate cap to go with the job—just short of a
jeweled crown.

Then in Korea there was his juvenile and frantic effort to
shed all blame for the disastrous advance on the Yalu, plus
his readiness to claim credit for Ridgway's accomplishment in turning a beaten army into an effective fighting
force.

It is not unfair, therefore, to suspect that there must
have been some vision of personal glory in his mind that
moved him in the end to envision an alliance among himself, Chiang Kai-shek, and Syngman Rhee that would result in his standing before the world as the White Knight
who finally slew the Red Dragon.

MacArthur's relationship with Chiang Kai-shek had
nothing conspiratorial about it, but surely there was more

to it than might meet the casual eye. It sometimes seemed to those who examined the relationship that MacArthur and Chiang dealt with each other as if they were in themselves two distinct, sovereign powers. Chiang, after he had fled to Formosa (Taiwan) with the Communists at his heels, developed a strong antipathy to the United States. The war lords who surrounded him (and perhaps ruled him) were so violently anti-American that they even threatened U.S.-trained Chinese officers in their command with instant demotion if they were heard expressing pro-American sentiments. John Osborne, writing in *Time* magazine on July 24, 1950, said that pro-American officers among the Chinese Nationalists "had their authority limited" and were threatened with "loss of their commands (and, some genuinely fear, of their lives)."

Osborne found this attitude perfectly excusable, in view of the failure of President Truman to compel his State Department to "abandon its equally debilitating and equally malicious attitude toward the Nationalist government." Osborne urged that MacArthur be given "full responsibility for all relationships, military and otherwise, between the United States and Nationalist China." And that would have suited Chiang and his war lords right to the final period. As a matter of fact, MacArthur, who was referred to by Chiang as "My old comrade in arms," managed to convey the impression to the Nationalists that he was a power quite apart from Truman and Company, so he was never included in the Nationalist distaste for all things American. And he was greeted as a friend and ally when he made a sudden trip to Formosa soon after the Korean war began.

The trip, described by MacArthur as "a short reconnaissance of [Formosa's] defense against possible attack," was made, MacArthur's devotees insist, on orders from Presi-

dent Truman. Truman gave no such order. The State Department had advised Chiang, however, that no final decision about the use of Chinese troops in Korea could be
made until General MacArthur's headquarters had conferred with Chiang about the defense of Formosa. The
Joint Chiefs then rather mildly suggested to MacArthur
that he not go in person but first send some of his staff to
do the conferring and appraisal. But MacArthur was not to
be denied this opportunity to dramatize his own determination to open a new front against Communism through an
alliance with Chiang. And dramatize it he did, with such
success that a *Time* correspondent noted that the Nationalist Chief of Staff General Chou Chi-jou "literally jigged
in delight."

For MacArthur arrived in Formosa with a party of
twenty, in two planes, carrying General Almond, Admiral
C. Turner Joy, General Willoughby, General Alonzo P.
Fox, who was Deputy Chief of Staff, Air Force General
George Stratemeyer and a flock of secretaries. And to mark
the occasion six Shooting Star jets, from the United States
forces in the Philippines, streaked across Taipei while
crowds of Chinese yelled with joy. The noted visitors
looked over defenses, conferred with their Chinese counterparts—and learned a number of things they did not include in their official reports.

According to *Time* magazine, they assured the Generalissimo that they would "expedite U.S. aid and set up a liaison staff" and that "coordination would probably include a
Nationalist armed-forces training program under U.S. officers." But they observed, according to notes made by General Almond, that U.S. aid was not always winding up
where it was meant to go. Tons of barbed wire, intended to
help make the shores impregnable against invaders from

the sea, were being used by the Chinese war lords to fence off their tomato gardens and their sweet-potato patches—to keep out, not Reds, but native Formosans. And in his discussions with Chiang, MacArthur received a surprising admission. When he told Chiang of the success of the Mac-Arthur program of turning over extensive Japanese farmlands to the peasants, Chiang said wistfully, "If I had been able to do that, I'd still be in China." And why had he not done it, his guest wondered. "The war lords," said Chiang, "wouldn't let me." Not the pro-Communists in the U.S. State Department, then, but war lords!

"MacArthur," Almond noted, "knew that Chiang was no democrat. But he was anti-Communist." And that, in those days of the alliance between Senators Taft and McCarthy, was all the qualification one needed to be elected to the "free world."

All the same, MacArthur, in furtherance of the Mac-Arthur foreign policy, declared aloud when he returned to Tokyo that he had completed arrangements for joint defense of the island and coordination of Nationalist and American military efforts to the end that the people of the Pacific should be "free—not slaves." If this seemed to portend a joint effort to bring the blessings of Chiang rule back to the benighted mainland—could MacArthur help it? He was simply, he explained, endorsing in his own way President Truman's declared intent to defend Formosa. And the President, after all, had just sent the Seventh Fleet there for that purpose. Truman had indeed ordered the Seventh Fleet to patrol the Formosa straits. But he had done so as much to keep Chiang from attempting any ill-advised invasion as to keep the Communists away from Chiang. And he had counted on MacArthur's emissaries to make that plain to the Generalissimo.

But the Generalissimo liked the MacArthur version better. According to John W. Spanier, who gives detailed and lucid coverage of this event in his book *The Truman-MacArthur Controversy and the Korean War,* Chiang Kai-shek issued a statement declaring that his talk with MacArthur had laid the foundation for "Sino-American military cooperation" and "more than implied that the 'American' in 'Sino-American' referred specifically to General MacArthur." Chiang wound up his own statement with the triumphant declaration that victory over the Reds was now assured. The uproar that followed extended from Washington to London, where the British announced their unwillingness to be bound by MacArthur diplomacy. The State Department requested William Sebald, their "adviser" to MacArthur, to fill them in on what had gone on in Formosa. But Sebald had not been there! MacArthur, on the ground that only military matters were to be discussed, had excluded him from the party. (Later MacArthur was to complain when he was not permitted to bring "his" correspondents to the Wake Island meeting.)

It seemed clear—to part of the world at least—that MacArthur and the State Department had adopted different foreign policies with regard to Formosa and Chiang. MacArthur, who could see what a hell of a mess was in the making, hastened to disown any "sinister" motives. But his explanation disingenuously indicated that he was just all mixed up by the bewildering changes of stance in Washington. If they would send forces to Korea to fight Communism, why not send them to China too? It is hard to grant that MacArthur was unable to grasp the meaning of what his superiors had been trying to convey to him, or that he did not realize as well as the next man the risks involved in monkeying with the switch that might ignite another world conflict. It seems far more likely that MacArthur knew exactly what he was doing and privately welcomed the onset of a worldwide onslaught against the Communist dragon. If he would get down on his knees to pray that the Chinese might enter the Korean War, why not pray for the jackpot?

President Truman, perhaps taking MacArthur's word about his bewilderment, promptly sent a delegation to Tokyo to help clarify the Administration's policy. Included were Averell Harriman, Special Assistant to the President; General Matthew B. Ridgway, Army Deputy Chief of Staff; and General Lauris Norstad, Air Force Chief of Staff. They looked over the state of affairs in Korea (where Harriman noted, he recalls, that General Walker seemed to be fumbling his job and that a man like Ridgway was badly needed). And they held long discussions with MacArthur, in which all three were impressed with MacArthur's grasp of his main task of building a working democracy in Japan. It was afterward reported by MacArthur biographers, and specifically by Lee and Henschel, that the Administration deliberately leaked a fable to the effect that Harriman had been sent to Tokyo to "rebuke" MacArthur. In a recent interview Harriman denied this emphatically. "Truman sent me to tell MacArthur to stay away from Chiang," he declared. "And there was no leak!"

MacArthur, Harriman said, agreed to support the President's policy toward Chiang, but offered this agreement "without full conviction." He weakened that conviction even further by promptly issuing a statement that, after insisting that his visit to Formosa was innocent of any political purpose or "anything else outside the scope of my military responsibility," went on to damn "sly insinuations, brash speculations, and bold misstatements" that were "invariably attributed to anonymous sources" but that really originated with people who "in the past have propagandized a policy of defeatism and appeasement in the

Pacific." And if anybody wondered who these people
were who had been doing the propagandizing, Senators
McCarthy, Taft, and a dozen right-wing columnists were
graciously pleased to identify them in the public press.

So Truman tried again, this time by means of a directive
from General Marshall's office to underline the fact that
any suggestion of a move against mainland China would
"carry the risk of precipitating a general war." Mac-
Arthur's response to this was snide enough to raise the
blood pressure of an even milder man than Harry Truman.
For MacArthur wired back that he understood the President's decision (through dispatch of the Seventh Fleet) "to
protect the Communist mainland."

Truman, however, let it go at that, and the Pacific wa-
ters seemed nearly pacified when MacArthur accepted an
invitation from the Veterans of Foreign Wars to send them
a message on the occasion of their annual encampment.
MacArthur did. He told them how heartily he endorsed
the President's decision to defend Formosa and then went
on to explain how valuable Formosa could be as a "ful-
crum" to our Pacific defense and to contradict those who
argued that counting Formosa as a part of "our defense"
might offend some of the people in Asia. Anyone who argued that way, MacArthur said, failed "to understand the
Orient." And from his own deep understanding of the Oriental mind (which had led him in 1939 to declare that anyone who thought Japan would invade the Philippines "did
not understand the Japanese mind") he allowed that
"nothing in the last five years has so inspired the Far East
as the American determination to preserve the bulwarks of
our Pacific defense. . . ." And he made it clear that he
looked on Formosa as a permanent bastion against possible trans-Pacific ventures by "a military power hostile to

the United States"—which could have meant only Communist China.

Inasmuch as President Truman had taken pains to make it clear to the Chinese that we had no selfish aims in Formosa, this belligerent statement sounded like a deliberate public dissent. And surely, unless MacArthur were deaf and blind to all that had been said and written to him and around him in recent weeks, he must have known that much. But, when Truman sent him still another expression of the official United States position on Formosa, MacArthur, with an air of injured innocence, insisted that he had done no more than proclaim his own devotion to Truman's plan to defend Formosa. And many observers are still convinced that this was MacArthur's sole intent.

These misunderstandings, some of which seemed so clearly deliberate, were to be magnified many times when the moment came to decide about sending forces into North Korea. Then both sides seemed to be prompted by motives they never would confess to. When General Ridgway reported to MacArthur at Christmastime in 1950, MacArthur complained that he was operating in a "mission vacuum." Indeed he was, for the State Department and the Joint Chiefs were guilty of a number of ambiguities, which MacArthur, in his "Who, me?" manner seemed overquick to take advantage of in order to press his own program. There was room for confusion, of course, in the fact that it was supposed to be the United Nations (minus the Soviet Union) that was directing the war. And the actions of the Chinese in first attacking in force, then yielding up prisoners and swiftly withdrawing increased the difficulty of reading their intentions.

One point seemed clear enough, on its face: the Joint Chiefs had certainly directed MacArthur not to use non-

Korean forces in the provinces bordered by the Yalu river. Their decision had been made clear to MacArthur at Wake Island. Yet MacArthur certainly paid no heed to this directive. In justifying his apparent dereliction, MacArthur pointed to a message from Secretary of Defense George Marshall, received only three days after the one that restricted his use of non-Korean troops. In this, Marshall assured MacArthur that "we want you to feel unhampered tactically and strategically to proceed north of the 38th parallel." By this time (September 30, 1950), South Korean forces were already operating north of the parallel.

Again it is difficult to believe that a conscientious commander, aware of his subordination to the civilian authorities at home, would have taken such ready advantage of this seeming contradiction. But MacArthur clearly never gave a thought to obeying the first directive. When some brash spokesman for I Corps (Milburn's command) announced in late October that all non-Korean troops would be halted forty miles south of the Yalu, there came a firm and prompt denial from MacArthur headquarters. And the very next day, lest there be further examples of speaking out of turn, MacArthur notified all his field commanders that he was "lifting all restrictions" on the employment of non-Koreans in the border areas. The Joint Chiefs, alarmed by this clear violation of their instructions, respectfully sought clarification from MacArthur—although one might have thought the seeking of clarification would have come from the other direction. MacArthur promptly explained that military necessity had caused him to ignore their orders, assured his superiors that he was going to take all precautions against provoking retaliation by the Chinese, and promised that this advance was going to wipe out all resistance in North Korea and bring the ultimate victory.

There must have been one or two in Washington who were more than slightly bewildered by this bravado, in view of the fact that a short time earlier he had warned the Joint Chiefs that the presence of a large body of Chinese troops "threatened the destruction of my command."

There had been confusion aplenty before the order to cross the 38th parallel was ever issued. By September 30, United States naval and air forces had been engaged for about two weeks in bombardment well above the parallel. In mid-August B-29s had dropped bombs on Rashin, a seaport close to the northern border, and other planes had bombed airfields and railroads along the Yalu, even venturing into Chinese territory to drop a few bombs (because of "poor visibility," MacArthur headquarters later explained) on the Chinese city of Antung, just north of the Yalu.

On September 15, the Joint Chiefs directed MacArthur to press this attack on the NKPA across the 38th parallel, to the end that the "destruction of North Korean armed forces" might be completed. And by September 30, when the main body of the Eighth Army had reached the mystical line, units of the ROK army, as has been noted, were already operating north of the 38th parallel. MacArthur however made a point of holding the rest of his force back to await a reply to a query he had sent to the Secretary of Defense concerning an order he planned to issue that would send Eighth Army in force across the parallel. Marshall promptly cabled him to proceed as planned "without further explanation or announcement," inasmuch as "our government desires to avoid having to make an issue of the 38th parallel."

But someone was making an issue of it at the United Nations, where our representative, Warren Austin, declared in a speech that the "artificial barrier" at the 38th parallel "has no basis for existence in law or in reason." Finally, on October 7 the General Assembly of the United Nations approved a resolution (suggested by the United States) that authorized the taking of "all appropriate steps" to ensure "conditions of stability throughout Korea," as well as to make it possible to hold elections, under U.N. auspices "for the establishment of a unified independent and democratic government. . . ."

There was, alas, no consensus in Korea as to the definition of *democratic*. To Rhee and his followers (General Hodge, in one of his last letters to MacArthur, referred to them as "Rhee and his gang of carpetbaggers"), *democratic* meant simply anti-Communist. To Kim Il Sung and his fellows, *democratic* was the name for what they practiced north of the 38th parallel. Many in the State Department had protested when, at the retaking of Seoul, MacArthur had restored Rhee to power. Rhee had been repudiated in the election that preceded the invasion and his grip on the presidency was tenuous in the extreme, requiring forcible suppression of his most ardent opponents.

All the same, it seemed clear that, if "stability" was to be restored to Korea and if, as the United Nations resolution required, free elections were to be held, then the Communist grip on North Korea had to be broken. MacArthur therefore translated this resolution as his authorization to drive clear to the Yalu, with *all* his forces, regardless of directives to the contrary. No one ever told him specifically that he could not do so, he insisted, for Marshall's directive that set him free "tactically" was enough to justify his disregarding the first order. Throughout his career, MacArthur had been adept at finding loopholes that left him room to do as he pleased.

But the people in the Truman administration were fond

of loopholes too. They had clearly suggested to MacArthur without telling him so in so many words, that he should go ahead and carry the war into North Korea and keep mum about it until after the United Nations had considered the resolution. And when it came time to dissociate themselves from MacArthur's disastrous effort to extend his government to the banks of the Yalu, they offered excuses of their own that bordered on the fatuous.

Despite the fact that the Wake Island meeting—at which MacArthur assured Truman that the Chinese were most unlikely to enter the war—took place a whole month *after* the directive was given to cross the parallel, there were some administration figures who argued that the crossing was a result of Truman's having been misled at the conference. But there never had been any hesitation on the part of the Administration to authorize the pursuit of the NKPA into their home territory. Nor, as Ridgway noted, was any specific order given to MacArthur by the Joint Chiefs to avoid contact with the Chinese or halt his reckless advance to the Yalu. He was told simply not to use non-Korean troops in the border area, and to press his attack on the Chinese only so long as there seemed a good chance of success. What commander could operate under a directive like that? At what point was he to decide that the contest was vain? That seemed almost as ridiculous an order as the one directing MacArthur to bomb only the *Korean* end of the Yalu bridges. It is reminiscent of the permission a gentle lady in Maine once gave to the lumber company—that they might fell the lower part of her trees but would have to leave the tops undisturbed.

It is almost too obvious that the Administration would have loved to earn credit for a triumph over "International Communism" while avoiding any blame that might derive

from a military defeat, as a football coach will sometimes
turn his back to let the quarterback make the choice of
play that will decide between victory and disaster. There
were few men in Washington who had been more ardent
than Acheson for a hot pursuit of the routed North Koreans, border or no border. He was no man to depend on the
United Nations or to let total victory slip away while he
awaited their approval. Justice William O. Douglas, in his
autobiography, quotes Acheson as saying, in 1979, "I never
thought the United Nations was worth a damn."

But the Administration at least, as Spanier points out,
had a clear political motive for seeking to associate itself
with a victory over Communism, what with the constant
sniping from the Taft-McCarthy combine. The papers and
the air waves in that day were full of charges of appeasement and betrayal, and MacArthur himself took frequent
occasion to point a righteous finger at the "forces of appeasement" that he seemed to believe infested the whole
Administration and probably even the White House itself.

MacArthur also persisted in "misunderstanding" the directives he received or interpreting them so liberally as to
render them meaningless. And while there was plenty of
room for bewilderment in the sometimes contradictory
orders sent out to him, he carried his pose of bewilderment
far past the point of credibility. He—and many of his admirers—insisted that he never for a moment believed the
Administration, which had allowed him to chase the People's Army across the border, would not grant him the
same privilege when it came to dealing with the forces in
that "sanctuary" across the Yalu. But he would have had
to be mentally deficient not to have understood, after his
exchanges with Truman, Harriman, and other administration figures, that the Administration—the authority he

was bound to obey—was dead set against igniting anything resembling a full-scale war with China. He might prate about there being "no substitute for victory" (a line he first used in a message to the West Point football team) but victory had a hundred different definitions. What sort of victory would it have been, had he involved our under-strength army and our dwindling air force in the occupation of a hostile land, alive with guerrilla bands that would almost certainly have harried us for a generation? The native Koreans, excepting the "carpetbaggers" in Syngman Rhee's entourage, would surely not have relished being turned into an outpost in a lifelong war against international Communism.

The Koreans sought a unified nation first of all, and unity could not have come about through imposition of the Rhee dictatorship on the North or the extension of the iron rule of Kim Il Sung to the South. There would still have been a struggle of the sort General Hodge and his successors had to cope with in the South, with "our" side insisting that there could be no such thing as a democracy that included any pro-Communists, and the other side taking the stand that "democracy" excluded all anti-Communists. Kim Kiu-sik, the "moderate" politician who might have led a coalition government in the South, had Rhee's carpetbaggers not blocked his path, had this to say in 1948 about establishing a free and independent Korea:

If we cannot unite, independence is impossible . . . our independence cannot come from war between the big powers or from peace among them. . . . It is obvious we can obtain independence only through our own efforts. . . . If we are going to be destroyed, let us be so by our own hands, and if we are going to be prosperous, let us be so by our own efforts.

[Quoted by E. Grant Meade, *American Military Government in Korea,* published in *American Civil-Military Decisions,* edited by Harold Stein.]

Of course our own definition of a "free" nation was an anti-Communist nation, so the freedom and unification of Korea were secondary aims with us, notwithstanding the ringing phrases in the United Nations resolution and in Dean Acheson's attempted justification of his views in the Senate hearings into the conduct of the Korean War. In those hearings Acheson very nearly matched MacArthur in fatuity. He kept dodging the issue of whether or not we *really* had meant to unify Korea by force and insisting that we had meant only to "round up" the fleeing North Koreans to make sure they would not come down and start the war all over again. He said, in answer to questions by Senator Harry Cain, that "we had the highest hopes that when you did that the whole of Korea would be unified." (Quoted by Spanier in *The Truman-MacArthur Controversy.*) And would that not have been uniting the country by force?

MacArthur, according to his bitterest opponents, had an unpublished motive of his own from the very beginning: He wanted to involve the nation in a full-scale war with China. But if that was truly his aim, his actions were Machiavellian to such an extent as to defy unraveling. MacArthur himself said that no man in his right mind would ever want this country to engage in a land war with China. And if he truly envisioned exporting the war across the Yalu into Manchuria and China proper, why did he tell his troops that the war was as good as over at Thanksgiving time? Why did he plan to string his attenuated forces along the whole length of the Yalu, when he had already declared he did not have troops enough to hold a static line across the narrow "waist" of the peninsula? Why did he tell Almond, his trusted Chief of Staff, that the war would be over by Christmas?

It was not until after he had thrown a scare into the Joint Chiefs with his talk of the "destruction of my command" that he set forth a list of recommendations that would surely have led to a wholesale widening of the war. It was then that he asked for the bombing of Chinese industry, a blockade of the Chinese coast, and the "unleashing of Chiang Kai-shek's forces"—which he himself had earlier agreed were not really combat-worthy. It almost sounded as if widening the war with China was the price he would charge for continuing the fight, for he insisted that, if his requirements were not met, the only alternative was withdrawal. Air Force Secretary Thomas K. Finletter called MacArthur's message blackmail.

When he set out to explain his views at the Senate hearings, MacArthur sounded as evasive as Acheson. For when asked what would follow if he did drive all the Chinese out of Korea through his methods, he could reply only that he did not believe they would "remain in a position of offensive action." Just how he arrived at such a fantastic conclusion he did not expound. It was the fruit, one suspects, of his transcendent understanding of the peculiar ways of the "Oriental mind."

It is no wonder, then, that unit commanders on the field were mystified by MacArthur's motives and that even the GIs were convinced that he must have had some secret understanding with the Chinese, as he pushed his reckless advance without regard for mounting evidence of imminent disaster. His self-confidence—that signal virtue that sustained him in his determination to proceed with the Inchon landing—seemed to have developed into a mania as he drove his scattered forces toward the Yalu, though they were short of proper clothing, lacked proper rations, and even were short on ammunition. He obviously courted disaster in both instances. At Inchon his luck (in which he seemed to have an abiding faith) delivered him. (As an example, given by Colonel Robert D. Heinl in *Victory at High Tide,* if the Russians who had packed the mines that were to be strewn along the channels of Inchon harbor had not forgotten to include the mooring harnesses, the first vessels of the attacking force might have been blown out of the water or left at ebb tide perched like rifle targets on the harbor mud.) In the home-by-Christmas drive his luck was unavailing.

Still, MacArthur did his utmost to fashion some sort of victory out of that humiliating retreat, while sedulously assigning blame for any failure to all those who had laid such unparalleled restrictions upon him. And when he was faced with the fact that a really competent army commander, who knew how to make use of much of the wasted firepower, who understood the need for a careful study of the terrain (where could tanks operate? where could streams be forded? what heights commanded the battlefield?) and who was adjusted to the idea of limited goals, could actually turn the U.N. forces around, he hastened to take credit for the decision to go on the offensive. Once more he became obsessed with total victory, which this time would naturally require a full-scale attack on mainland China. What moved him now? Why would he at this point contemplate a war that he had earlier implied only a madman would engage in?

It hardly seems possible that he could have been urged by any motive so petty as the desire to wipe his own record clean, regardless of the price in lost lives. Yet when one considers the feverish manner in which he often strove to maintain unblemished his own image of infallibility, this possibility does emerge.

It surely was altogether alien to MacArthur's nature to leave a smear on his record as hideous as the one he had earned by his end-the-war offensive, if there was any way that it could be worked off. It must be borne in mind that MacArthur as well as Truman had a strong political motive for keeping his escutcheon unblemished: He had never abandoned his dream of adding the final diadem to his fame with election to the Presidency. Despite his public disavowals, his intimates knew that this remained his secret goal, provided it could come to him as nearly as possible by acclamation. The day after MacArthur left Tokyo to return to America, General Almond's wife wrote to her husband and expressed the hope—which, she said, many in Tokyo shared—that MacArthur might return some day as President of the United States.

It is conceivable too that MacArthur might have been moved by jealousy of Ridgway's success in turning the Eighth Army into a victorious fighting force, after MacArthur himself had deplored the collapse of its morale and insisted it would have to be withdrawn if it could not be reinforced. This feat of Ridgway's was, to many a fighting man, a miracle the equal of Inchon. MacArthur, however, actually belittled Ridgway's accomplishment and his avowed determination to destroy the enemy's forces. This sort of fighting, said MacArthur, was merely conducting an "accordion war" in which one side pushed ahead until its line of supply became attenuated and the other, closer to its own source of supply, grew stronger and reversed the process, continuing thus to the point of stalemate.

But what other sort of fighting did MacArthur envision,

after he had, by his own lights, "sprung the trap" that forced the Chinese to attack "prematurely"? Did his strategy not include the resumption of the offensive? If so, his field commanders never knew it. General Walker, on the very day of his death, promised I Corps that "this magnificent army" would be safely withdrawn from Korea. And if there was no intention to fight more than a rear-guard action against the Chinese, what was the advantage of "springing the trap"? Thousands of lives might well have been saved by seeking a parley then and there. If the trap-springing was not a fairy tale then the rejection of an "accordion war" was a mental aberration.

There was, however, one more "secret plan" to be unveiled before MacArthur and his acolytes ran out of argument. General Courtney Whitney, MacArthur's alter ego, declares in his book *MacArthur: His Rendezvous with History* that the plan was devised early in 1951. William Manchester, in *American Caesar,* reports that this scheme was outlined in a cable to the Joint Chiefs at that time but curtly rejected. These may be solemn truths, but no record has yet been published to verify them. The sources given by Manchester as authority for his assertion do not bear him out. MacArthur, in his testimony before Congressional committees on the conduct of the Korean War, never mentioned the plan. The plan, in brief, was this: MacArthur, after bombing all enemy installations south of the Yalu into the ground, would sow a field of radioactive waste along all the routes by which the Chinese might escape from the Korean peninsula or reinforce their armies engaged there, and then would, with the aid, preferably, of Chiang Kai-shek's forces, stage a gigantic, two-pronged amphibious attack—a double Inchon—that would demolish the Chinese armies and bring the war to an end.

Persistent as MacArthur was in presenting his standard plan of achieving victory by carrying the war into China and destroying her warmaking potential, it seems strange that he never publicized this further scheme—which, wild as it was, at least had the virtue of complying with the Administration's aim of confining the war to Korea. And because the plan is presented in detail first in Whitney's book, then—in almost exactly the same words—in MacArthur's autobiography (which most authorities believe was written by Whitney anyway), in the middle fifties in an interview with Hearst reporters, and finally in a 1962 memorandum from MacArthur to Eisenhower, one is permitted to suspect that this is just one more example of the Monday-morning quarterbacking that was much in vogue after peace was made in Korea.

But before peace, or even a truce, could be arranged, MacArthur made the move that earned him his dismissal. Crudely, deliberately, with complete understanding of what would ensue, MacArthur undertook to sabotage Truman's effort, in March 1951, to open peace negotiations with the Chinese. Even though MacArthur and his sycophants, in typically disingenuous and mealymouthed fashion, insisted he acted in all innocence, no one not blinded by hero worship could overlook the arrogance and contempt with which MacArthur deliberately flouted Truman's directive. Taking advantage of his advance knowledge of Truman's imminent call for negotiation, MacArthur trumped the move by issuing his own call for unconditional surrender. In his threadbare "Who, me?" style he pretended, of course, to be merely uttering a "military assessment," then couched his assessment in such deliberately inflammatory terms that rejection by the Chinese of the implied invitation was, as of course he knew it would be, inevitable. All he asked was that the Chinese admit their complete defeat, their utter inability to mount and support a military effort equal to our own, and their vulnerability to a full-scale assault on their homeland by our air (and, by implication, our atomic) power. What nation ever, short of complete destruction, agreed to "negotiate" an unconditional surrender?

Truman had notified MacArthur on March 20 that he was about to announce his willingness to discuss with the Chinese terms under which the fighting could be brought to an end, and he asked MacArthur to indicate what steps might be needed to give him the freedom required to ensure the safety of his troops and the maintenance of contact with the enemy while discussions among the allies, preparatory to truce talks, continued. MacArthur in reply asked simply that his forces should have no further restrictions placed upon them. He then promptly set about contriving his own proclamation—the sort of statement, he afterward insisted, any field commander had a perfect right to issue when he was ready to meet the enemy and accept his surrender.

But this was no military assessment or mere invitation to talk terms. It was a taunting belittlement of the enemy's warmaking ability, a threat to carry the war right into the enemy's heartland, and a flamboyant prediction of the enemy's complete humiliation. Knowing full well that his civilian superiors at the Pentagon and at the United Nations had no such program in mind, MacArthur even threatened that "a decision by the United Nations to depart from its tolerant effort to contain the war to the area of Korea through expansion of our military operations to his coastal areas and interior bases would doom Red China to the risk of imminent military collapse."

Who in God's name, an angry President might have

asked, ever equipped this man with the authority to countermand United Nations' decisions in a manner so highhanded as this? Obviously our American Caesar had grown so great on the meat of imperial power that he believed he could fashion foreign policy on his own. And certainly he had usurped the President's constitutional right to direct the armed forces and to formulate foreign policy. Yet, no matter how he may have seethed inside, Truman swallowed his anger for a time. He boiled over only when MacArthur, perhaps certain now that he had Truman on the run and could count on the willingness of a rapt Congress to endorse the MacArthur agenda of widening the war, sent a letter to the Republican Minority Leader, Congressman Joseph Martin, that directly attacked the President's policies.

MacArthur, typically, characterized both these acts— the call for surrender and the letter to Martin—as "routine." The tone of injured innocence in *Reminiscences,* where he described this controversy, is almost disarming, or would be, were it not for the strong suspicion that his head courtier, Courtney Whitney, selected the phraseology. The original call for surrender, or acknowledgment at least of the hopelessness of the Chinese cause, is described in *Reminiscences* as a "routine communiqué" which he had "prepared to be issued from Tokyo before receiving" from the Joint Chiefs the message that Truman was planning his call for truce talks.

MacArthur was aware, of course, that what he terms a "muzzling order" had been sent to him, reminding him that no "speech, press release, or other public statement concerning foreign policy, military policy, or other public statement should be released without clearance from the Department of the Army." MacArthur had promptly started playing games with his superiors by pretending to believe that every routine communiqué had to be cleared with Washington, and he began to send such petty stuff immediately, only to be told that such reports were not worth bothering with. And quite naturally, he asks his readers to believe, the call for surrender was just another "routine communiqué."

His letter to Martin too, in which he spoke of fighting "Europe's war with arms while diplomats fight it with words" and where he strongly endorsed the utilization of Chiang Kai-shek's troops in Korea, was prompted, MacArthur asks us to believe, by the fact such a response to a Congressional inquiry "has been the prescribed practice since the very beginning of our nation." And MacArthur, clearly, would be the last to deviate from a prescribed practice. As for the publication of the letter, that just mystified MacArthur. Martin did it, MacArthur vowed, "for some unexplained reason." One deduces that MacArthur was amazed to see the letter in print. For it made it sound as if MacArthur wanted to "spread the war" by dragging in Chiang's troops when "I only wanted to end the war . . ." —there being, of course, "no substitute for victory."

At the time all this took place, however, MacArthur's counterfeit innocence was more than his President could take. Even a more saintly man than Truman could ever have been might have succumbed at this point to an urge to grab the General by the scruff of the neck and shake some manners into him. But Truman held his peace, or bottled his anger, until he had received from the Departments of State and of Defense and from the Joint Chiefs of Staff a unanimous decision that MacArthur would have to go.

The manner in which MacArthur was informed of his dismissal has been deemed by most observers as unduly blunt and heartless. For he received word of it at second hand, after it had been announced on public radio. But the bluntness had not been intentional, regardless of what Whitney and MacArthur said afterward. The message was first sent to Frank Pace, at the American Embassy in Seoul. Pace, who was to deliver the message to MacArthur in person, was at the front and could not be reached immediately. When no acknowledgment arrived from Pace, Truman, fearing (with good reason) that the news would very quickly be leaked to the press, had Bradley send a direct message to MacArthur. It arrived, unhappily, after the news had already been broadcast.

The various versions of the General's receipt of the news all picture it as a shock and a surprise. Whitney tells how "MacArthur's face froze," when the word was whispered to him by his wife at the luncheon table. And MacArthur (or perhaps Whitney again) in *Reminiscences,* with typical exaggeration, declares that "no office boy, no charwoman, no servant of any sort would have been dismissed with such callous disregard for the ordinary decencies." Many a servant might have told him differently.

But in truth MacArthur was not by any means taken unawares. He owned a direct pipeline of some sort to the Pentagon and surely knew what was afoot. When General Almond, taking a brief respite from the battlefield, visited MacArthur in Tokyo, the day before word came of his dethronement, he found MacArthur unusually disconsolate. When Almond bade his chief goodbye, MacArthur responded:

"I may not see you any more, so goodbye, Ned."

Almond, telling the story in his 1975 debriefing, recalled that he protested that MacArthur had frequently come to see him in Korea, so why such a farewell?

"I have become politically involved," are the words Almond recalls MacArthur using. "I may be relieved by the President."

Obviously MacArthur had learned that he had once more misjudged the strength of the "enemy at home," or had overestimated that of his own forces and that his gamble had been lost. It is especially interesting to note, in view of MacArthur's wide-eyed insistence that his statements were all offered from a strictly military point of view, that he knew full well he had been involved in a political maneuver.

One of MacArthur's biographers mourned the General's failure to receive the sort of honors from the "enemy" that Napoleon had been offered on his way to exile. But MacArthur was not on his way to exile. He was going home to campaign for the Presidency. And his departure was marked by a spectacle as magnificent as any that city had ever seen. General Almond's wife described it in a letter to her husband:

> From the gates of the Embassy to the doors of the plane, all six miles, there was a solid line of guards. Japanese police, soldiers, sailors, and marines. And behind them thousands lined the streets the entire way.... Everywhere he moved, people applauded, everywhere he turned, eyes followed him, some weeping, some silent, and some I am sure, among the followers of Acheson, relieved. When he turned from the seventeen-gun salute, his eyes were wet, as when he spoke to me. At other times his eyes were quiet. But I did not see him smile ... the passengers boarded the plane and the MacArthurs stood waving from the top. A roar of "Bonsai!" went up from the Japanese in enthusiasm and love for the man who had saved them and their emperor and their country....

There is no question that in his role as emperor-in-being, MacArthur had been a complete success. He played this part better than any other he had ever undertaken. He was aloof, unafraid, generous, firm, and carried himself with a long-practiced air of nobility. He had shown himself a man of peace, without vindictiveness, and he had helped unleash and direct the strong democratic forces long at work in Japan. Although his chief contribution to the process had been to prod the participants into action and to insist on a clause outlawing the creation of a military force in Japan (a clause which was promptly disregarded), MacArthur had promoted a constitution for Japan that provided a permanent base for the creation of eventual democracy. And most of the Japanese were truly worshipful.

Like their emperor, MacArthur permitted no intimacies and recognized no peers. He refused to leave the Embassy to bid the Emperor farewell, so the Emperor had to come make his manners at the Embassy. MacArthur never moved out among the common people, never entered a Japanese home. To many plain people in Tokyo he was a god and the movement of his gleaming Cadillac along the way from the Embassy to the Dai Ichi building always gathered a throng of worshipful spectators. A number of Japanese women even invited him to come father a child for them, so that the divine lineage might be preserved in the homeland. (MacArthur, according to Dr. D. Clayton James, did father a child many years before in Mexico, a child he never acknowledged.)

MacArthur seemed uncertain of his welcome in the United States, perhaps unsure now of just how powerful a force Truman commanded. But his welcome was hysterical, wherever he traveled, with cheering admirers to meet, and even mob, his plane and to line the sidewalks along his route. In New York, his welcome outdid the Lindbergh greeting, which had first set the standard for a New York welcome-home parade. MacArthur appeared before Congress to deliver a speech he had been saying over to himself for hours. (Indeed, whole paragraphs of the speech had been used years earlier in a talk to an American Legion convention.) And his closing "Old soldiers fade away" theme was soon echoing all over the nation.

MacArthur however had no intention of fading away. According to Courtney Whitney, MacArthur was prompted by his sudden realization of the way the nation was deteriorating to set out to halt the downhill slide by a series of talks. In violation of Army regulations, he held on to the plane that had been assigned to the Supreme Commander of the Allied Powers and employed it until his Congressional appearances were ended. Meanwhile, Mrs. Matthew Ridgway, who had been slated to use the plane, which was now assigned to her husband, to fly to Tokyo to join General Ridgway there, sat without transportation in lonely quarters in Washington, until finally General Marshall, taking note of her plight and despairing of ever getting the plane back from MacArthur, let her use his own plane for the trip.

But before MacArthur committed himself to a personal-appearance tour that was a thinly disguised campaign for the Presidency, he revealed still one more plot that he had uncovered among his enemies in Washington. There had been, he averred, a plan concocted among the appeasers and pro-Communists in the State Department to turn Formosa over to the Red Chinese and then to take Red China into the United Nations. He had personally thwarted this plot, he declared, by sabotaging the peace efforts of the President. He was by this time, of course, no longer pretending that he had been wholly innocent in issuing that "military assessment." Instead, he was taking full credit for saving the nation from betrayal by those who might, in today's terms, have been described as a "Gang of Three"—Truman, Acheson and Marshall. And he found consolation of a sort in a fairy tale that had been whispered to him sometime earlier—or that perhaps he had invented. When he said goodbye to his successor, General Ridgway, he told Ridgway:

"I have it on good authority that Truman is suffering from an incurable brain disease. He won't last six months."

5

the price of glory

Douglas MacArthur was a fluent and persuasive, although somewhat grandiloquent talker, who loved the sound of his own voice. When more than two or three were gathered together to listen, he would, adopting a platform manner, give out with pear-shaped platitudes and pomposities that, while occasionally striking the simple solemn, would prompt some of his listeners to groan inwardly. General Oliver Smith of the U.S. Marine Corps, included in one MacArthur audience just before the Inchon landing, walked out on the performance and declared himself fed up with the theatrics. Admiral Doyle, a more forbearing man, allowed that MacArthur could outdo the Barrymores.

Like most professional talkers, MacArthur treasured certain well-sculptured sentences and happy metaphors, and he used them over and over again, until the juice was nearly wrung out of them. Already quoted has been the line that became his trademark, "There is no substitute for victory!" which he first used to help a cheerleader egg the

Army football team on to triumph. "Old soldiers never die," borrowed from a British army ballad, became the MacArthur theme song. His biographers, Lee and Henschel, report that he used this phrase often in letters to ailing colleagues. And he made frequent use of a paragraph he had discovered on a war memorial in his wife's home town, Murfreesboro, Tennessee, and adapted to his own purposes: "I do not know the dignity of their birth, but I know the glory of their death."

Another favorite, which MacArthur was likely to present as a quote from a dying soldier, from a worried Korean comrade or from an influential Asian politician, was "Don't scuttle the Pacific!" He invented that one himself.

In his writings, particularly in those he felt were destined to be preserved in history books, MacArthur sometimes strove so hard to attain rhetorical heights that he lost his footing. He was devoted to superlatives—". . . the greatest military achievement in all history!" (the Red Army's success in driving the Germans from the gates of Moscow); "without precedent in military history" (the restrictions under which he had to conduct the Korean campaign); "the greatest defeat of the free world in modern times" (giving up any portion of North Korea to the Chinese Communists); "No more subordinate soldier has ever worn the American uniform" (about himself). Now and then he even misused a word in a way that would have made his elementary-school teacher wince, as when, for instance, he used "prevaricate" as a transitive verb. (In his decision affirming the death sentence for Japanese General Homma, he wrote that "to hold otherwise would be to prevaricate the fundamental nature of the command function.")

In his writing, MacArthur, like many politicians, sought resonance by seeking complex ways of expressing simple thoughts, as when he wrote on at least two different occasions about the code that distinguishes between "those things that are right and those things that are wrong." Similarly empty phrases fluff out much of his public expression, with the result that readers and listeners were often more overawed than enlightened.

MacArthur also fancied himself as a religious leader, even though his attendance at church, at least in his active years, was less than spasmodic. He seemed to take special delight in reciting prayers aloud provided he might lead whatever congregation the Lord provided. Sometimes he would attempt this under circumstances that were just short of alarming. When, during the Second World War, an officer arrived with a message from Admiral Nimitz denying MacArthur the battleships he had asked for, MacArthur promptly called upon those present to join him in reciting the Lord's Prayer. When he ceremoniously reinstalled Syngman Rhee as President of the Republic of Korea, at the retaking of Seoul, MacArthur again caused many a colleague to squirm in embarrassment when, disregarding the fact that here Christianity was a minority religion, he invited the assemblage to follow him in recital of the Our Father, his own voice sounding above all others in the rolling, tremulous tones of an old-time revivalist.

One of MacArthur's favorite bits (in the vaudeville meaning of the word) might have been named the "dying-dove" bit. He would employ this as he expounded how the American's fear of death contrasted with the Oriental's calm acceptance of his fate. As if he were performing on a school stage, MacArthur would accompany the production with expansive gesture, dramatic crescendo and diminuendo, and finally by closing his eyes, letting his head droop gradually to his chest, slowly bringing his hands to-

gether beneath his chin, and allowing his voice to fade to a
whisper as he completed his act with the lines "he folds his
wings like a dove ... and ... di-i-i-e-e-e-s." His audience of
subordinate officers would at this point often exchange
quick glances pregnant with comments none dared express.

MacArthur indeed did not hesitate to invite frequent
public acclaim for his concern for the numbers of men who
might die while serving under him. He took pains to contrast the losses suffered under Eisenhower at the Battle of
the Bulge with the far fewer lives that were lost in his own
campaigns in the Southwest Pacific. Yet he more than
once urged his commanders to push on toward an objective
without reckoning the possible loss of life. And, as Dr.
James points out in his authoritative *Years of MacArthur,*
the casualties in the Papuan campaign, where MacArthur
ordered his commanders to finish the job regardless of cost,
were one killed out of eleven troops in action, compared to
Marine and Army losses at Guadalcanal (outside Mac-
Arthur's sphere) of one in thirty. Yet MacArthur did not
gag in describing the Papuan losses as comparatively light.
Dr. James quotes him as declaring that "probably no campaign in history, against a thoroughly prepared and trained
army produced such complete and decisive results with so
low an expenditure of life and resources." But many wit-
nesses to the contrary could no longer testify. Of those living who had witnessed the slaughter in that campaign, a
large number, after hearing MacArthur belittle the sacri-
fice, developed a contempt for the theater commander that
lasted all their lives.

Comparing the fighting in the Southwest Pacific with
that on the Western front was difficult anyway, some military observers have pointed out, inasmuch as the fighting
in the Pacific was often spasmodic, whereas that on the

Western front continued day and night. Even so, there were other spots than Papua where MacArthur paid little heed to the cost in blood, reckoned against the relative un-importance of the objective. He pushed an unremitting at-tack on strongly defended positions on the island of Negros in the southern Philippines at great cost, although the is-land itself had no strategic value. But none of these adven-tures compared in pure recklessness with his advance on the Yalu in 1950, with hopelessly divided and improperly equipped forces. In commenting on this operation one em-bittered senior commander said later, "MacArthur cared little for the common soldiers under his command—nor for the officers either."

MacArthur, however, in writing of this campaign in *Reminiscences* offers a comment so sanctimonious that even some strong stomachs found it difficult to ingest:

> I myself felt we had reached up, sprung the Red trap, and escaped it. To have saved so many thousands of lives en-trusted to my care gave me a sense of comfort that, in com-parison, made all the honors I had ever received pale into in-significance.

Many lives were saved indeed, not by springing the "Red trap," the existence of which none of the field commanders had ever doubted, but by the failure of the Chinese to press their advantage immediately. The Chinese apparently had not been prepared for such a prompt collapse of so great a part of the United Nations line and so did not pursue as avidly as many American commanders expected. The Eighth Army, during the first part of the retreat—at least as far as Musan-ni—after the early panic in the rear eche-lon, withdrew in good order, although without any plan to make a stand. And along the route, which was illuminated by the flames of burning villages, the troops were able to count casualties that were never reckoned in the official figures, for they were mere civilian refugees, desperately hurrying away, as refugees always do, from whatever army was moving toward them. General (then Colonel) John Michaelis still recalls the scene vividly:

> ... literally millions of refugees, blocking the road by sheer mass, the silent columns moving without hope, shelter or food, avoiding others' tragedies of death, loss of total possessions, and those who simply sank to the ground too tired and defeated to move; the tossing away of babies, borne on their mothers' backs, frozen to death. . . .

Ultimately, civilian casualties were counted as 240,000 dead, as compared to 140,000 American soldiers killed in action. But the civilian figure is still considered too low by many Koreans, and it does not include the many hundreds of thousands of innocents killed in North Korea, where the United Nations air forces managed to demolish totally so many towns and villages that General Emmet O'Donnell of the Air Corps eventually complained there was nothing left to bomb.

Destruction of dwelling places anywhere within reach of our fire power was deemed a necessity, because any structure might provide shelter for enemies. And often houses were hit simply because they made such tempting targets. General Almond proudly recalls in his diary how he selected a village within range of his artillery and requested a "fire mission" to burn the village down with 105-mm. white phosphorous shells. It took only eleven minutes, he notes, between the time fire was requested by the forward observer and the starting of several fires in the village. He used this measure to judge the efficiency of other artillery units with similar missions.

But thousands of people too were continually being

caught in the cross fire between the opposing forces. There
had never before been a major war quite like this, in which
battle lines were so unstable, with first one side and then
the other sweeping through the countryside at such unbe-
lievable speed. First the North Korean People's Army sped
almost unopposed from the 38th parallel to the Naktong
river while terrified countryfolk scattered before them.
Hardly any of the farms and villages along the way had
had any more warning than the sudden roaring of the great
guns as they rolled closer and closer. The leaders of the
ROK forces had no time to give thought to the civilians
along the route of retreat. Indeed they afterward expressed
dismay at their failure to round up and carry along the
thousands of young males who had not yet been put into
uniform—and who were soon drafted into the ranks of the
invaders.

Then, after Inchon, the legions of Kim Il Sung dispersed
with almost equal swiftness, to escape the closing jaws of
the trap, and hastened northward almost to the very border with Manchuria. To stay clear of these lightning
marches was almost impossible in Korea, where roads were
narrow and few—and largely off limits to civilians after the
war began. Plain people owned no transport and usually
carried all their goods on their backs. There were trains,
but they were not for the poor. When ordinary Koreans
had to travel by train they usually wished they could have
walked. Colonel Frank H. Britton, a member of the
U.S.-U.S.S.R. Joint Commission in Seoul before the war,
tells of seeing men, women and children being loaded, at
the Chong-ju railroad station, into "freight cars unfit for
human beings" and "packed like animal crackers in a card-
board box."

In consequence, there were often frantic noncombatants
cowering on disputed ground, with guns going off all

around them. And many, of course, became casualties that were never counted.

When the retreating South Korean army crossed the Han river, in the first evacuation of Seoul by the only bridge available, the South Korean demolition squad dynamited the bridge while it was still jammed with people, including some American correspondents. *Time* correspondent Frank Gibney described the scene (*Time,* July 3, 1950):

> . . . Traffic moved quickly until we reached the bridge. There the pace slowed, then stopped . . . We got out of the jeep and walked forward to find out what was delaying traffic. The milling crowds of civilians pouring over the bridge made that impossible. We returned to the jeep and sat waiting. Without warning, the sky was lighted by a huge sheet of sickly orange flame. There was a tremendous explosion immediately in front of us. Our jeep was picked up and hurled fifteen feet by the blast. My glasses were smashed. Blood began pouring down over my head. Crane's face was covered with blood. I heard him say, "I can't see!" . . . The Korean army command had panicked and blown the bridge too soon. The demolition squad, instead of roping off the bridge at both ends, incredibly told only the traffic in the middle what was about to happen. . . All the soldiers in the truck ahead of us had been killed. Bodies of dead and dying were strewn over the bridge. Scores of refugees were running pell mell off the bridge. . . .

But other Koreans were killed somewhat more deliberately by their fellow countrymen, sometimes in furtherance of a private feud which war provided an opportunity to reignite and sometimes "legally" by the army or the police—whose chief task before the war broke out had been to eliminate "communism," in cooperation with right-wing "youth groups," some of whose members were well past their youth. There is no reckoning the number of innocents who were eliminated in North Korea as collaborators. Inasmuch as almost any person who had received an advanced education or who had achieved community standing in business or in a profession must have "collaborated" to the extent of having acknowledged the fact that one had to get along with the Japanese, it was a fairly simple matter to do away with one's private enemies on patriotic grounds.

In the South, under the Rhee dictatorship, which MacArthur had insisted on restoring, all sorts of people who had followed the Communist party lead or who had even associated themselves with Communists in some left-wing organization and had then experienced a change of heart, were enrolled in an organization called Po To Mang—or "information society"—as an indication of their rejection of Communist doctrine. When the Republic of Korea army reentered many a village that had been temporarily lost to the North Koreans, they more than once or twice simply gathered together all the Po To Mang and machine-gunned them. Obviously they were "security risks."

The New York Times on July 13, 1950, printed a Reuters dispatch from Korea that reported twelve hundred "communists and suspected communists" had been executed by the South Korean police since the outbreak of hostilities (on June 25). Kim Tai Sun, chief of the Korean National Police said that those executed had been considered "bad security risks" and had been shot on his orders in Seoul and "other towns in the battle area".

On August 21, 1950, John Osborne wrote in *Time* magazine about "The Ugly War":

To attempt to win [the war], as we are now doing in Korea is . . . to force upon our men in the field acts and attitudes of the utmost savagery. This means not the inevitable savagery of combat in the field but savagery in detail—blotting out villages where enemy might be hiding; the shooting and shelling of refugees who may include North Koreans in the anonymous white clothing of the Korean countryside, or who *may* be screening an enemy attack upon our positions.

And there is savagery by proxy, the savagery of the South Korean police and (in some sectors) the South Korean Marines upon whom we rely for contact with the population and for ferreting out hidden enemies. I am not pretending to issue righteous indictments—or to ignore the even greater savagery of the North Korean army. I am simply stating the elementary facts of war in Korea, the South Korean police and the South Korean Marines whom I have observed in the front line areas ... murder in order to save themselves the trouble of searching or cross-examining them. And they extort information ... by means so brutal they cannot be described.

Just how much of this ugliness penetrated to the austere and telephoneless office on the fifth floor of Tokyo's Dai Ichi building from which MacArthur was, as he put it, "running the war," no tongue now can tell. But MacArthur did, early in the conflict, send a radio message to North Korea's Kim Il Sung, and drop the same warning by leaflet, declaring, after he had heard of the shooting of American prisoners of war, that "these crimes are not only against the victims themselves but against humanity as well. I shall hold you and your commanders criminally responsible under the rules and precedents of war." There is no record, however, of his ever having uttered a similar warning to the South Korean Marines. In December 1950, *Time* printed this report:

Since the liberation of Seoul last September, South Korean firing squads have been busy liquidating "enemies of state"—Korean civilians accused of sabotage or collaboration with the Communists. With savage indifference, the military executioners shoot men, women, and children. Some people said that more than 700 civilians had fallen before the guns of ROK troops. Others said the total was at least 800. Last week in Seoul while US and British troops expressed their loathing at the wholesale slaughter, three American clergymen—a Methodist and two Roman Catholics—made a formal protest.

Major General Lee Ho Viu, Vice Chief of South Korean Martial law headquarters, insisted that no one had been executed without due process of law. Civilians sentenced to death, he said, were supposed to be hanged. "But we have found shooting by firing squad more convenient."

Harold L. Ickes, Secretary of the Interior under Franklin Roosevelt, in the *New Republic* of March 1951 quoted a long dispatch that Gene Symonds of United Press had filed from Korea on January 16:

... The handsome young Korean woman lay sprawled beside the road into Osan. One breast was bared to the winter wind, and her arms were frozen in the position she held her baby. Next to her in the snowbank was the baby, swaddled in rags, its frozen face peering out.

The mother and child were only two of the many refugees killed along the road leading into battered Osan which American forces captured Monday. Bodies of refugees had been dragged to the side of the road ... some spots where the snow and frozen blood had melted were turning brown.

Blankets and children's clothes, bits of clothing and small tots' articles were strewn along the road in confusion. At one place I saw a tiny, red baby cap with something in it in the mud. I did not see the baby.

Some of the refugees were frozen to death. Others were ripped to pieces. One man, or woman—I couldn't tell which—dressed in tattered clothes, looked like a cotton-stuffed doll that had been chewed by a playful puppy.

This stretch of road was strafed several days ago on a report by air observers that Chinese Communist soldiers were shedding their uniforms and mingling with columns of refugees.

I didn't see any soldiers yesterday. That of course does not mean they were not there. . . . I don't know. This was just one spot on one road in Korea. There are many more that I haven't seen.

Perhaps a few Chinese or Korean Communists were killed. I hope it was worth it.

On May 28, the *New Republic* carried another report from Korea, written by a former Korean official who had traveled from Pusan to Taegu soon after the recapture of Seoul in 1951:

. . . A month before my visit, the Kochang area had been the scene of a particularly brutal massacre by South Korean troops who accused the village of Shin-Um of harboring Communist guerillas. The trouble started the evening of March 6 when the Reds attacked Shin-Um for the fourth time. Since the village had been occupied three times before by Communist guerillas, the South Korean Army concluded that the villagers supported Communism and supplied the partisans with food. The army said that when the loyal troops re-entered the village, they discovered "the villagers were cooking food for the Communist partisans. Some were singing loudly the song of the North Korean Communist Republic!"

According to the National Assembly, the retaliation against the villagers was "merciless and indiscriminate." South Korean troops shot anyone who resisted arrest.

Under pressure of the National Assembly, President Rhee

eventually ousted three cabinet members . . . on the grounds that the publication of the Kochang massacre report damaged the prestige of the government.

Some 1400 tenant farmers had lived in Shin-Um before the incident. At the time of my visit not a villager remained, and about half the straw-and-mud houses had been razed. . . . Any houses left standing were occupied by the South Korean troops and police. . . .

In the shifting scenes of war the [Korean] villagers live in terror of both sides. They complain that when Communists invade a man's home at night his wife is in no position to refuse to cook rice for them. Yet she may well be executed by the loyal army or police the next morning as a supporter of the Red guerillas. . . .

Gregory Henderson (*Korea: The Politics of the Vortex*) gives a more vivid version of what may have been the same incident. He relates that the villagers, several hundred of them, including a number of women and children, were called together by a South Korean army officer acting under orders, on the pretext that they were to

hear an order. On assembling, they were sprayed with machine-gun fire from prepared positions, and wiped out. The Assembly committee sent to the spot to investigate was ambushed by the ROK forces and retreated. Even a decade later, feelings were so bitter that . . . after the fall of the Rhee regime, the villagers seized the man who had then been police chief, spread-eagled him, piled leaves underneath, poured oil from a local rice mill, and roasted him as . . . in summer they roast a dog.

Henderson also tells of another event, typical of the corruption of the Rhee dictatorship: A National Defense Corps was recruited, in the winter of 1950–51, from the many thousands of young men who had fled south in fear of the Chinese Communists. The Corps numbered half a million and was to be financed largely with millions of American dollars. But the money was grabbed and pocketed by the Rhee minions, to be used for bribing assemblymen and other politicians, or just for feathering a private nest. As a result, many units in the Corps went as long as two weeks without food, thousands suffered from exposure and (according to the estimate of the Provost Marshal General) several hundred starved to death or died from the freezing weather.

Besides these major horrors, there were small-time atrocities repeated in villages both north and south that added more nameless hundreds to the list of uncounted casualties. While the well-schooled revolutionaries who formed, at least in the early days, the vanguard of Kim Il Sung's armies, had been taught that the populace provided the sea that they must swim in and so must be treated with kindness, the later draftees were under no such restraint. And as the armies surged back and forth, leaving friends and enemies behind, there were always private scores to be settled in every province. All through the contested area, parents trained their little ones to greet passing jeeps or marching soldiers of any hue and under any banner, North, South, Chinese, Korean, or Occidental, with shouts of *"Mansei! Mansei!* Long Live!" But noncombatants, under no discipline from above, once their side was in charge, could avenge themselves patriotically on rivals of any sort. But all such petty vengeances were of little account compared to the slaughter wrought by the strafings, the bombings, the burnings, and the forced exposure to starvation and brutal cold.

At home in the United States, and even eight hundred miles away in Tokyo, people who bothered to read about such matters undoubtedly counted them all as but the fortunes of war, to be preferred in all degrees above the loss of American lives. Still, there was squeamishness in high places at laying too much emphasis on the nonsporting aspects of the struggle. When General Ridgway, a man given to calling everything by its right name, designated his contemplated offensive as "Operation Killer," some hands in the Pentagon were raised in horror. It was *extremely* bad public relations, a few men gasped, thus to flaunt the unpleasant side of the struggle. Better, apparently, to allow the citizenry to go on believing that war is just an oversize football game, with the laurels falling at last to the stoutest hearts.

The Rhee dictatorship, however, owned no heart at all. Its one aim was to extend its rule, at any cost and by any means, over the entire nation and to concentrate on building the Rhee fortune, enhancing the Rhee prestige, and bolstering the Rhee power. The Assembly, strongly rightwing, came up with a constitution that was a sort of hasty fusing of the American and British forms that created a powerful president, yet one to be chosen by the Assembly, and a prime minister whose function was largely ceremonial. This constitution, known for a time as the "excerpted constitution" because it had selected bits and pieces from Japanese, American and British models, offered all the basic human rights, or seemed to. It did not guarantee them however, for in order to implement any of them, laws had to be passed to define their application. No such laws were passed while Rhee held his veto power. And the constitution did give him a special right of his own—to rule by decree in an "emergency." He also held the right to dismiss all ministers, including the prime minister, when it suited him to do so.

The voters who elected the Rhee-dominated assembly,

Henderson has made clear, had not voted for any special interests of themselves as a class or party (except perhaps land reform), but had voted because they had been told to do so by the local authorities, because they were caught up in the excitement of the great holiday, or because they were eager to send a favorite local boy to the big city. And the Rhee government had no dedication to either the form or the goals of democracy. Politics, to them, was the getting and receiving of favors and the bettering of one's station as rapidly as could be managed.

Emergencies arose rapidly in the period preceding the war. In the early years, Rhee was greatly strengthened by the creation, at the behest of the military government, of a police force named the Community Protective Association manned by young "patriotic" (i.e., right-wing) volunteers, who served merely for the "honor" of being able to "keep order" in the villages. Their chief function, however, seemed to be to terrorize left-wingers. They also helped persuade the villagers to participate in the election that was to lead to Rhee's election as president. After that, the police forces became the only really cohesive political "party" in South Korea.

In 1949, when the Assembly began to feel its oats and actually managed to pass a land-reform bill over Rhee's veto, Rhee arranged for the murder of his chief rival, Kim Ku, former head of the "Provisional Government," himself a right-winger, the only candidate who had run against Rhee for the presidency. (He had received 16 votes in the Assembly to 180 for Rhee.) The assassin, tried and convicted of the murder, was promoted by Rhee from lieutenant to lieutenant colonel. In short order, sixteen members of the Assembly had been arrested, jailed and tortured.

By the time the war broke out Rhee had the Assembly

thoroughly cowed and was in complete charge of the nation, through his police force and the extensive Japanese-type bureaucracy that discouraged all local political activity while the police and the "volunteers" ferreted out every sign of "leftism."

General Hodge had never had any illusions about Rhee; MacArthur, if he did not know exactly what sort of "democracy" Rhee practiced in Korea, must have been purposely keeping both eyes and ears closed when Korea was mentioned in his presence. MacArthur's admirers all insist that Korea was none of his concern once the State Department had taken over in 1948. But MacArthur, although he certainly ignored what was happening there, never yielded up all his authority. In July 1948, in response to a message about Hodge's leaving his job, MacArthur sent Hodge a message that included the line: "It is assumed that any changes in existing command relationships will maintain the channel for this authority through CINCFE. . . ." CINCFE, of course, was MacArthur.

The depth and the breadth of corruption under Syngman Rhee was almost more than one individual could grasp. The number of bureaucrats increased threefold under Rhee, with almost every man in the whole fraternity busily peddling favors of one sort or another and hastily stuffing his own purse against the day when he would have to move out and let some other favorite get his own beak in the gravy. Just what the system looked like from close up was revealed in a report written in September 1960, by an infantry captain (in the United States Army) named Sae Jick Park, who was an aide to Frank H. Britton, Commanding General of the 1st Cavalry Division.

Part of Park's report follows. The spelling and the grammar are his own:

For a decade Shingman Rhee regarded himself and has been regarded as the only ruler in Korea. He was despotic, stubborn, and self-complacent. In a sense he might be called a stupid fool who would never listen to any true advise and never look into a newspaper to see the life of the people either. For example when Shingman Rhee stopped into a department store to learn the price of merchandise, a treacherous underling compelled the merchant to decrease the price below the current value. The deceived Rhee was pleased with the low cost and consequently purchased several items.

Shingman Rhee can hardly escape from being called a villain of trick and plot if one knows the facts of Patriot Kim Koo's death. The deceased Kim Koo, a great patriot who endeavoured to achieve the unification of Korea, was almost certainly assassinated by Rhee's instigation. Otherwise the assassinator Duhi An would not have been promoted to the rank of full colonel and given "a good job" from which he could draw big money. It is beyond irony that the people have held an annual mourning ceremony for the Patriot whose murderer has been living in prosperity. The late Mr. Soungju Kim, one of the harsh critics of Rhee's government, was shot by a subordinate of General Won, then Provost Marshal, in compliance with orders contained in a secret letter of Shingman Rhee.

It is well known that Rhee was virtually isolated from the people and the world by dishonest followers within his own party. The most notorious follower was Kiboung Lee, the former speaker of the National Assembly, who, being ill-advised by his American-educated wife, exerted all his efforts to become Rhee's successor. He had directed the so-called political hoodlums, a hidden organization which had deep roots in the society and constantly harrassed the people. He is said to have been the ringleader of an unsuccessful assassination attempt on John Chang, the former vice-president, Lee's most formidable rival. Besides these terrible crimes, he was considered the symbol of graft and corruption. Finally, Kiboung Lee ended his life in a suicide pact with his family. [He suffered from advanced syphilis.]

What made matters worse was the Liberal Party's self-glorification of their own party. Without regard to the millions of unemployed and the low standards of living conditions of the people, they were lavish in spending more than 3 hundred million hwan in building the statue of Shingman Rhee in Namsan Park, Seoul, Korea. Very recently it cost the Korean people one million seven hundred thousand hwan to dismantle.

The people would no longer allow the villainous politicians and police force to rig the elections in favor of Kipung Lee and the Liberal party. This resulted at first in an uprising in Masan, which prompted the student's demonstration of Korea University on April 18 [1960]. The police attempted to oppress and appease them by using the hooligans.... This did not stop the uprising but instead instigated the joint demonstration of the students of Seoul National University and others....

In Seoul, the masses of people got completely out of control, and police fired into the crowds of outraged students and citizens who were protesting against the dishonest and corrupt election campaign. [Won by Rhee and Kibung Lee.] The situation became more intense as people were inspired by the courage of the students facing injury and death by police gunfire. They marched beyond the barricade to the Kyong Mu Dae [the Korean "White House"] and demanded the overthrow of Rhee's Liberal party. Their demands were complied with and a new government was established. Goodness knows, if the students had not been willing to die at Kyong Mu Dae, decency and democracy would have perished throughout Korea.

And goodness also knows how many lives might have been saved had MacArthur followed the State Department's urging that he *not* reinstall the monstrous Rhee in the presidency when Seoul was retaken after the Inchon landing.

Of course, the original mistake was made when MacArthur accepted the estimate (by General William Roberts of the Korean Military Advisory Group) that the Korean defense force was the "best doggoned shooting army" and that they could handle anything that North Korea might throw their way. MacArthur also vastly underestimated, as he so often did, the strength of his opponents. He did not expect any tanks and, soon after the invasion had already begun, told correspondent Marguerite Higgins, "Give me two American divisions and I can hold Korea" (*The War in Korea,* p. 33). Almost immediately after that, his requests skyrocketed until, before he was relieved, he was asking for a Field Army.

But almost all his moves, after Inchon, would cost the United Nations forces dearly in blood. His decision to split his command and transport X Corps via sea to Wonsan choked off supplies desperately needed by Eighth Army. Even Korean military leaders found this move inexplicable. Generals Hyong Kun Lee and Chung Il Kuon, in interviews with Dong-A Ilbo in 1978, agreed that MacArthur made a serious mistake in separating X Corps from Eighth Army. Said General Kuon: "As the Chinese Communist forces entered the war, the lack of cooperation between the Eighth Army and the X Corps exposed a critical weakness." And Lee added: "The X Corps obviously should have been placed under Walker's command."

And Vice-Admiral James H. Doyle, the man who directed the Inchon landing and the man, too, who would be charged with performing the miracle of the Hungnam evacuation, believed then and believed until he died that the way to take Wonsan was by the overland route.

"My opinion," Doyle recalled, "of the logical way to take

Wonsan was to attack overland via the road connecting the
objective to Seoul. Organized North Korean resistance had
disintegrated, South Korean forces were meeting token resistance as they drove north along the east coast and I believed—and still believe—that logic dictated an overland
move. . . ."

General Ridgway concurred. In his book *The Korean
War,* Ridgway wrote:

> Whatever the arguments in favor of another Inchon-type
> assault on Wonsan, they did not outweigh the importance of
> closing the trap quickly on the fleeing North Koreans. There
> was a good highway and rail line—bombed and battered it is
> true—overland from Seoul to Wonsan through one of the
> relatively level stretches of the peninsula. The forces put
> ashore at Inchon could have moved with reasonable swift-
> ness up this road, north and east to Wonsan, to link up with
> forces driving straight up the east coast. This would then
> have closed the gate on the rapidly fleeing enemy and left
> him no time to regroup and refresh his forces.

The really dismaying aspect of this decision by Mac-
Arthur, that was to cost so dearly in time and blood, was
that there is strong reason to believe it was made, not for
military advantage at all, but for strictly private reasons.
More than one officer close to the situation was convinced,
and remained convinced, that MacArthur either hoped to
provide his favorite, Almond, with an opportunity for glory
(such as he had been denied in World War II), or sought
simply to avoid placing Almond in a position subordinate
to General Walker, a man Almond despised.

Even General Chung Il Kuon, quoted above, made note
of the fact, in this connection—"Almond was MacArthur's
man," he observed. "Walker repeatedly asked Collins, the

Army Chief of Staff, to place the X Corps under his command, which fell on a deaf ear because of MacArthur's intervention."

Doyle too remarked on this aspect of the decision. After noting MacArthur's expressed lack of confidence in Walker, Doyle volunteered:

> But I believe the resistance of Major General Edward M. Almond, Tenth Corps commander, to being subordinated to Eighth Army was a stronger factor than lines of communication or General Walker in bringing the sea move on Wonsan. Almond strongly pushed for a sea lift to Wonsan, in my opinion, because he knew he had no possibility of retaining his independent command if Tenth Corps moved on shank's mare to Wonsan.

By the time the "home-by-Christmas" plan had developed, Almond's command was very nearly the equal of Walker's, with only one fewer U.S. division than Eighth Army owned and two fewer South Korean divisions. Operations of both commands were directed and coordinated from Tokyo, so Almond and Walker were on the same command level. And on February 15, 1951, Almond finally received his coveted third star. Men under his command who had been forced to withdraw in the face of overpowering enemy attack had to wait a long time for either promotion or decoration. One officer who sought recognition for a unit commander in his group was told that decorations were not given for retrograde movements.

The reckless advance on the Yalu that cost both X Corps and Eighth Army so dearly and wrought such murderous destruction on the Korean population was another move that could not be justified on military grounds. When Eighth Army was ordered to advance, Colonel Paul Freeman's 23rd Regiment was already heavily engaged with an identified Chinese regiment, forty miles south of the designated "line of departure," yet was ordered to break contact and move north to "spring the Chinese trap"—as the MacArthur fairy tales subsequently explained.

General Walker, in command of Eighth Army, was dismayed by the order. As General Ridgway tells it in *The Korean War,*

> General Walker well knew that he lacked the force and the equipment for a sustained offensive against an enemy whose numerical superiority now seemed clear. He sent a straightforward message to Tokyo acknowledging AN AMBUSH AND SURPRISE ATTACK BY FRESH, WELL-ORGANIZED AND WELL-TRAINED UNITS, SOME OF WHICH WERE CHINESE COMMUNIST FORCES.
>
> The eventual response from Tokyo was, however, one of irritation and impatience at Walker's failure to move forward on schedule.

Marine General Oliver Smith, it has already been noted, also made an effort to have his orders reviewed by higher authorities, and for this Almond later hinted that Smith was simply afraid to be the first one to contact the enemy. Yet had General Smith been even half as reckless as Almond, he might well have lost the entire 1st Marine Division. Whether Almond would have been awarded his third star, notwithstanding such an unmitigated disaster, is still uncertain. As it was, in his debriefing, Almond unblushingly took part of the credit for the foresight and foot-dragging that enabled General Smith to stage his brilliant attack-to-the-rear that brought his forces out whole and still combat-effective.

Casualties at Inchon might have been far higher—even

to the point of aborting the landing—had Almond been able to bulldoze Admiral Doyle out of meeting with Mac-Arthur to ask for some naval bombardment to reduce the enemy fire power. Because, regardless of what Almond or MacArthur may have imagined, Inchon harbor was well-defended by gun emplacements on Wolmi-do (Wolmi island) and Observatory Hill, guns that might well have destroyed the landing craft. Two days of naval bombardment silenced most of them and rendered the assault that much safer.

MacArthur's lack of interest in the "details" of the landing, reported to Doyle by General Almond, is effectively illustrated by a passage in *Reminiscences,* where MacArthur brags of his success in outwitting the enemy. Describing the approach of his ship, the *Mount McKinley,* into Flying Fish Channel, MacArthur says: "Then I noticed a flash—a light that winked on and off across the water. The channel navigation lights were on. We were taking the enemy by surprise. The lights were not even turned off." What MacArthur did not know, but almost everyone else in the special planning group did, was that the light—in a lighthouse on Palmi-do, indicating the channel—had been turned on by Lieutenant Eugene F. Clark of the United States Navy, head of a raiding and reconnaissance party that had managed to climb into the lighthouse and repair it, so that it could be turned on at midnight, when the assault vessels would be near. (The story of this Hairbreadth-Harry adventure is set forth in vivid detail by Colonel Robert Heinl in his book, already mentioned, *Victory at High Tide.*)

MacArthur's detachment, that often cost his forces so dearly, extended far beyond his lack of interest in details of planning, of terrain, and of logistics. He also managed to ignore, early in his dealings with Korean matters, at least two specific and ominous warnings that must have crossed his shining desk in the Dai Ichi building long before the fighting began. One was the warning given by Arthur Bunce, mentioned earlier, that forecast civil war if we were foolish enough to continue to support the Rhee faction. The other was an even more ominous note sounded by General Hodge while he was still in command of the U.S. Armed Forces in Korea. On September 29, 1947, Hodge sent a long message, via Tokyo, to the War Department. This, of course, was transmitted through MacArthur's headquarters, with a copy for MacArthur's desk. The message dealt mainly with the Soviet proposal for early withdrawal of all occupying forces from Korea. The last paragraph read:

> If now after the Soviet proposal, we should build up a strong army in South Korea, we are setting the stage for full scale civil war in this area—with the non-Communists facing the odds of a two-year start by the Communists. Our decision must be made based on overall foreign policy. If we decide to build a South Korean Army, large scale support in supplies, transportation, arms, and equipment must be forthcoming soonest from sources beyond local jurisdiction.

MacArthur, of course, was not the only one who ignored the warning in this message from what would become the battle zone. The Truman Administration was just as bent as MacArthur was on building an anti-Communist strong-hold in Korea. Given the Soviet desire to establish a friendly nation on its borders and the United States' urge to plant an unfriendly one there, it may well have been too late to apply the brakes to the wheels of history. But Mac-Arthur, while supporting the creation of a South Korean army—which was soon dubbed a "Constabulary"—argued against providing it with proper strength, feeling that, if any muscle was to be added anywhere, it should be added to the Japanese police.

Essentially, what was at work, both in Washington and in Tokyo, was the notion that foreign policy should be based, not on political, but on strategic considerations. Formosa, which had originally, but quietly, been conceded to the Red Chinese as historically a part of that nation and undefensible anyway, became, under the new Iron Curtain policy, a potential bomber base, as did all other islands within our Pacific "defensive perimeter." And Indochina, as well as Korea, was to be "defended" against takeover by leftist, even though indigenous, forces. MacArthur, in his hare-brained plan to liberate Java with two Australian divisions and reestablish the Dutch regime there, was actually anticipating the Iron Curtain policy by some five years.

Victor Purcell, a Cambridge University lecturer who was attached to MacArthur headquarters during the Pacific Campaign in World War II and was later a colonel on the staff of Lord Mountbatten, commented on "strategists" in a letter to the editors of *The New Republic* in February 1951: ". . . strategists are, in my long experience, whatever their eminence as navy, army, or air force officers, usually politically immature. Indeed, it not infrequently happens that a brilliant commander has the political development of a boy of 14."

Many who were unfortunate enough to listen to some of MacArthur's political rantings during his ill-starred campaign for the Republican Presidential nomination in 1951, would have allowed that this would be an overstatement in MacArthur's case.

Purcell also commented on the power of the military missions: "I heard frequently of the strategical indispensability of Formosa to the United States. As if possession of a bombing base could offset the bitter enmity of 500 million Chinese!" Most Americans would not have agreed that, in deciding to play on Chiang Kai-shek's side, we were earning bitter enmity from all the mainland Chinese. Our foreign-policy makers usually were happy if they won the friendship of the "better people" of a foreign land—the college-educated, professional, entrepreneurial, and land-owning class, even though the multitude that had suffered under the war lords, or some similar oppression, might remain disaffected. The great masses, after all, as in the Teddy Roosevelt lexicon, were people who were "born to be governed"—and who better qualified to govern them than the kind of people who, in a symbolic sense, "could talk our language?"

It was always difficult to believe that any mass of people anywhere could actually hate us, as well-disposed and honorable and charitable as we knew ourselves to be. Unfortunately our condescension sometimes put the lesser folk off, once they had got in the habit of considering themselves our equals. Acheson's effort to mollify the Chinese by using our relationship with Canada as an example of how well we understood the job of respecting other people's boundaries merely set Chinese teeth on edge, so much did it sound like the head-patting effort of a Church of England bishop to assure some restless millworkers that they did not need to go out on strike to win "fair play."

One oddity of our colloquy with the Red Chinese, before they sent their troops into Korea, was that, at the very time we asked them to accept our heartfelt assurances that we meant them no harm, we were ridiculing their own very

specific threats of intervention as mere Communist bluff.
Even when the Indian Ambassador to Peking, Sardar Pan-
nikar, had reported that the Chinese would indeed enter
the war if the United Nations drove into North Korea, our
policy makers, as well as MacArthur, named him a simple
stooge for Stalin and so not worthy of attention. Stooge he
may well have been. But that was no reason for failure at
least to take heed of the threat. MacArthur treated it with
utter scorn as merely a scare tactic designed to cheat him
out of certain victory.

Privately, MacArthur, in view of his early avowal of
hope that the Chinese *would* intervene, may simply have
been trying to dissuade the State Department and the
Joint Chiefs from trying to slow down his precipitate advance. Perhaps he already smelled the complete destruction of Red China's warmaking power that he later assured
listeners he could have achieved.

For some reason, hardly anyone who has reported Mac-
Arthur's "secret plan"—apparently revealed only after he
had been relieved of his command—has made note of its
utter indecency, not to say insanity. The notion of creating
a radioactive zone in North Korea was apparently first
broached by Senator Albert Gore of Tennessee in 1951. At
that time President Truman and the Atomic Energy Commission, on whom the plan was urged, simply ignored it—
as they probably ignored a hundred crackpot suggestions
every week.

How could any person in complete control of his facul-
ties ever have contemplated such a scheme? Spreading
"atomic waste" wholesale along a wide belt of countryside
would not have been like spreading manure in a cornfield,
or sand on a sidewalk. The very process would have been
indescribably hazardous, requiring safeguards not yet

dreamed of. And once the villainy had been accomplished, immeasurable damage would have been wreaked on living things for miles in every direction, as winds and water-courses picked up the deadly offal and scattered it without regard. Not only would the land where it was applied remain lethal to all life for the better part of a century, but slow death and horrid deformity would have lain in wait in a thousand places all over the entire area.

If MacArthur really did cook up such a plan, involving such wholesale destruction of plant, animal and human life, and did not merely offer it as a might-have-been to prove how close he had been to victory, then he must have put about as much thought into it as he would put into scratching his head. For if it had "worked" it would have succeeded only in disgracing the United States throughout history.

Although a number of writers have reported that Mac-Arthur never contemplated the use of the atomic bomb against Koreans or Chinese, he did, in the years after his leaving Tokyo, speak of atomic bombing as an option that our "appeasers" failed to make use of—or failed to allow him to make use of. Of course, in describing how he would destroy China's warmaking power, he included air and naval bombardment too. But actually he did not seem to have given particularly deep thought to this project either, for he apparently believed that there were war industries in mainland China that could be wiped out by bombing. Actually, China's "warmaking" potential lay largely inside the Soviet Union, and not even MacArthur was so lost to common sense as to advocate opening an atomic war against that nation that would have meant the immediate loss of all of Europe.

William Manchester in *American Caesar* records that

the off-the-record interview MacArthur gave to two reporters, Lucas and Considine, representing the Scripps-Howard and Hearst papers respectively, in which MacArthur detailed his "atomic waste" plan, was released at the time of his death in 1964 regardless of the fact that MacArthur had, as long before as 1957, changed his mind about atomic warfare.

That may well be true. But in a letter to Brigadier General F. R. Zierath, Chief of Staff of the Alaska Command, in September 1960, MacArthur wrote very aggressively of the fact that our political leaders "lost their courage when, with our control of the air and the seas, our virtual monopoly of the atom bomb, and with half a million fresh troops offered by Generalissimo Chiang Kai-shek, we could have destroyed Red China's capability of making war and assured her pacifism for a century to come." This seems to indicate quite clearly that at least he had not been reluctant to use the A-bomb when we had a "virtual monopoly." And he did not in any way, in this letter, qualify his interest in use of the bomb.

(It is worth noting that, in December 1951, when General Almond had, as he put it, been "kicked upstairs" to Commandant of the Army War College, he engaged in correspondence with the Army Chief of Staff, General J. Lawton Collins and Karl Bendetsen, Assistant Secretary of the Army, concerning the tactical use of atomic weapons. In a letter to Bendetsen, he wrote: "I feel that we do have a definite requirement of promptness, reliability, fidelity and accuracy of delivery of atomic weapons on the battlefield in close proximity to our own troops which can be met now only by artillery delivery. Therefore we should step up the delivery date of the first group of guns. . . ." Whether MacArthur ever knew of this study is not known. Almond did note that "Headquarters Far East Command this year reported its unreadiness to use atomic weapons on or near the battlefield because of inadequate information and instruction at all levels of command.")

To judge from this letter to General Zierath, the size of the forces on Formosa had grown, in a few months, more rapidly than the dimensions of a fish in a fish story. In the beginning, MacArthur had talked of 30,000 troops. Later it became 60,000. And even he had agreed at the start that the troops would not be of much help in their current state of readiness and their removal would greatly weaken the defenses of Formosa. But now, in 1960, he recalls that there were half a million "fresh" troops available in Chiang's domain. One wonders where they came from, and by what magic they had been freshened.

But MacArthur's recollection was often hazy and his use of figures—like his reading of the enemy's mind—careless in the extreme. In an interview with gathered reporters (*The New York Times,* December 2, 1950), after the sudden Chinese incursion had put a disastrous end to his "home-by-Christmas" offensive, his intelligence officer, General Willoughby, imparted to newsmen the fact that MacArthur had "gambled" that the bulk of the Chinese forces would never cross the Yalu. But at Wake Island he had set forth as a solemn truth that China had only 60,000 troops that they could put across the Yalu, and even those would be slaughtered as fast as they hit the Korean shore. Actually, as Lieutenant General Alfred M. Gruenther informed the Senate Armed Services Committee a few days after the retreat, there were 260,000 Red Chinese troops already in Korea before MacArthur's "gamble" was even undertaken.

(Once the entry of the Chinese could no longer be de-

nied, MacArthur was not above inflating the size of their
forces, as he sometimes inflated the number of "fresh
troops" available in Formosa. When he was busy trying to
"blackmail" [Finletter's word] the War Department into
letting him make use of Chiang's forces plus four National
Guard divisions from the United States, he declared that
"one million, three hundred thousand Chinese troops" had
been sighted advancing on Korea. Admiral Forrest Sherman, Chief of Naval Operations, commented: "If there are
that many Chinese, their supply lines must run all the way
to Shanghai.")

But careless gambling with human lives seemed to be
second nature to MacArthur, who apparently assumed
that he knew the truth by revelation, and not by searching
out the facts. In his address to Congress, after his relief by
Truman, MacArthur told how victory had been within his
grasp if only he had been permitted to bomb mainland
China, use the troops from Formosa, and turn the Navy
loose on the Chinese coast. But under questioning he revealed not only a complete ignorance of the strategic situation but a lofty disdain for the truth.

When Senator Brien McMahon of Connecticut asked
him what right he had to gamble the country's entire military strength on his faith that wholesale attack on China
would not ignite a World War, MacArthur airily replied:
"Everything that is involved in international relationship
amounts to a gamble."

"But how," the Senator persisted, "would you defend
the American nation in that war?"

"That," said MacArthur, "does not happen to be my responsibility."

All he planned to do, he explained, was disrupt China's
ability to "supply the sinews of war to their armies in

Korea." When another Senator gently reminded him that most of the "sinews" came from Russia, he simply denied that such was the case. He also went on to paint a picture of the workings of the Chinese "processes of distribution" that had about as much relation to obvious fact as the tales of Hans Christian Andersen. "The slightest dislocation in the normal processes of distribution," he propounded, "and you might well have fifty million people starving at one time." At that time, China was shipping a million tons of grain to starving India by way of Dairen.

MacArthur, just before he was relieved, had assured two Congressmen, according to Washington newsman Tris Coffin, that war between the United States and China was inevitable and that we must therefore strike the first blow before the Chinese grew stronger. MacArthur's intelligence officers then confided to the Congressmen, who were visiting Tokyo, that there was no hint at all that there would be any move by the Soviets in retaliation for a move against China inasmuch as there were no Russian troops in Manchuria.

But Truman had already been warned not only that there were indeed two units of Russia's Far East Air Command in Manchuria but that heavy submarine concentrations had been reported at the southern end of Sakhalin Island, within easy reach of Japan. Nationalist Chinese intelligence, Coffin recorded, also sent word of fifteen Russian divisions in Manchuria. Still, inasmuch as definite identification of Chinese divisions known to be in the Chinese order of battle had not deterred MacArthur in his helter-skelter plunge to the Yalu, it hardly seems likely that, had he been given his head, news of imminent Russian intervention would have slowed him down. The result might well have been destruction of most of our defensive

strength. But that, of course, would not have been Mac-
Arthur's responsibility.

In his campaign for the Presidency, which his sycophants insisted was merely an effort to "wake up
America," MacArthur, as has been noted, no longer made
any bones about the fact that his offer to talk to the Chinese—the move that had wrecked the President's truce
plan—had been a deliberate effort to do exactly that. He
bragged to the American Legion that, by heading Truman
off this way, he had prevented a major act of appeasement
that would have turned Formosa over to the Red Chinese
and brought Communist China into the United Nations.

After the Russian-Chinese breach, historians began to
point out that there had never been much of a threat that
Russia and China would gang up against us anyway.
(Acheson, before the split was even hinted, had predicted
the development of Titoism in China.) But there was every
reason to believe that the Chinese and the Russians were
working closely together at the time MacArthur was calling for an all-out attack on the mainland (by sea and air).
United States intelligence had already reported the existence of a secret treaty between the two nations that committed China to the defense of the hydroelectric plants on
the Yalu from which power was transmitted as far as Port
Arthur. And the Soviets were operating munitions plants
in Manchuria that were vital to their own military
strength. It hardly seems possible that the Soviets would
have sat and watched as these plants were demolished by
our air attacks, whatever ideological differences may have
been developing between the two dictatorships. And Russia was as much concerned about the establishment of an
anti-Communist beachhead on her own Far Eastern borders as China was.

Of course, the opening for MacArthur's highly successful attacks on the "appeasers" at home was provided by the Administration's own lack of a Korean policy that could be articulated in common-sense terms. In the beginning there *had* been a determination (soon disavowed) to unite all of Korea under one government. And Acheson particularly clung to the hope that a signal defeat of world Communism might be obtained, even though the Administration dared not demand it. Instead, they simply urged MacArthur to wreak some sort of notable damage on the Communist cause, without naming any specific objective—when failing to achieve it might have laid the blame for a major defeat on their own backs.

Exactly what was to be won in Korea nobody ever could say. Even had the Chinese not come in and North Korea been finally subjected, there would still have been a generation of civil conflict there that might have bled us white. For Korea is still no place to mount an offensive, or even to establish a defensive stronghold. And at this time there is precious little freedom there, either in what we try to pretend is an outpost of the free world or in that make-believe "democracy" that Soviet Russia has bequeathed to the people of North Korea. What MacArthur and the Truman Administration sought there ultimately was glory of a sort—either the prize of the Presidency or eternal immunity from the shame of being thought soft on Communism. And the price was paid by both the gallant and the ungallant dead.

6

---

the real macarthur

There was one endearing, even redeeming, quality in Douglas MacArthur that many who met him never knew he possessed. That was his ability to shed, like an overcoat, his aloof, imperious, often icy manner and become—in the presence of a few good friends or well-disposed strangers—unaffected, humorous, concerned, even warmly affectionate. He would exchange mild jibes with favored colleagues, pay close heed to questions, inquire sympathetically into another's woes, perhaps share a few of his own. Even at such times, however, he allowed no undue familiarity. He remained always the father figure, or at least the head of the household. Vice-Admiral James Doyle enjoyed telling of the time MacArthur, a passenger on Doyle's flagship on the way to Inchon, came to join the Admiral's mess. Doyle, sitting, as his rank decreed, at the head of the table, stood up and pointedly indicated to MacArthur the honored chair at Admiral Doyle's right. MacArthur, just as pointedly, ignored the Admiral's gesture, stalked to the

opposite end of the table, and took his seat there. Admiral
Doyle savored a silent chuckle, recalling the tag line of an
old joke: "Where Murphy sits, *that's* the head of the
table!"

With his family too, MacArthur set his public pretense
aside. General Whitney describes the manner in which
MacArthur, when his boy was small, would get down on
the nursery floor with his son, or march about in make-believe military formation as he and the little boy kept step
to the "Boom! Boom!" of an imaginary drum. MacArthur's
dependence on his wife Jean was plain for all to see, particularly when, on the return from a meeting in Korea, Mac-
Arthur would fretfully search the crowd at the airport and
keep asking: "Where is Jean?"

With correspondents too, MacArthur liked occasionally
to strike a one-of-the-boys pose, if he could do so without
letting down his guard. Once, on his way to Korea, with a
parcel of writers, MacArthur pulled a corn-cob pipe out of
his pocket and declared, with a laugh, "I would not dare
smoke this in Tokyo. They'd think I was a farmer." All
present dutifully laughed with him, although many of
them must have known that MacArthur had a half-dozen
such pipes in his Tokyo office and smoked one whenever it
suited his mood.

As a matter of fact, MacArthur often, like most people
who are deeply concerned with the impression they are
making, would go to surprising lengths to curry a little approval from his companion of the moment. Once he even
made a startling confession to Major General George C.
Kenney of the Air Corps, a man he much admired for his
zeal and ingenuity in putting together the indispensable
Fifth Air Force that became MacArthur's right arm in the
South Pacific. When he was Chief of Staff, MacArthur told

Kenney, he had probably done as much to damage the Army Air Corps as any man in history by blocking its development as an independent force. Of course he more than made up for this early dereliction by his extensive dependence on air power in the Southwest Pacific. In Korea, he carried his penance to the point of wildly exaggerating in some of his forecasts the ability of air power to interdict the battlefield.

MacArthur never did see fit to confess, however, that he had done equal damage to the development of an armored force. Machines, to MacArthur, were just substitutes for the horse and needed no special cultivation. In 1928, before anyone had heard of a Panzer division, Major Adna Chaffee organized an experimental mechanized force, but was prevented by MacArthur from continuing his experiments. According to Dr. D. Clayton James, MacArthur's insistence on decentralizing the mechanization program was the chief reason, in the eyes of military authorities, why the American Army fell so far behind the major European armies in the development of armored-warfare tactics.

The flaw in MacArthur's character that aroused the most anger among his colleagues and the men under his command was his habit of bearing false witness. The complicated falsehood he invented to justify his disastrous "home-by Christmas" offensive in Korea was perhaps his most outrageous. But the MacArthur communiqués from the Southwest Pacific during World War II were notoriously misleading in their constant implication that MacArthur was right at the front and in their frequent corruption of the figures covering enemy and friendly casualties and equipment losses. One man in Washington who handled many of these messages was so incensed by the unremitting exaggeration and outright falsification that to this day he cannot mention MacArthur's name without bitterness.

Dr. James, in *The Years of MacArthur,* offers notable examples:

After the Battle of the Bismarck Sea on March 3 and 4, 1943, MacArthur reported 10 Japanese warships and 12 transports sunk or sinking, 55 enemy planes destroyed and an uncounted number damaged, while 15,000 enemy troops were either drowned or killed, with hardly a survivor. MacArthur set Allied losses at a single bomber and 3 fighter planes, with a few damaged but able to return to base.

Because Air Force headquarters was skeptical of this report, it started an investigation of its own. And when the war was over and the matter was still in dispute, the Tokyo headquarters of the Far East Air Force conducted a further investigation, using Japanese records and testimony of Japanese participants. This investigation substantiated what the first had discovered, that only about 2,900 Japanese had been killed, not 15,000, and that only 12, not 22, Japanese warships had been sunk. MacArthur refused to accept either report and insisted only that, in the future, the sources for such contradictory information be identified to him so he could take "appropriate action." The Official Air Force history accepted the report of its own investigators. But no copy of the Tokyo report ever reached Washington, merely the notes of an Air Force officer who had read the report in Tokyo. MacArthur headquarters, it was whispered, had ordered the report destroyed. MacArthur also filed a false report on another action, the raids on Rabaul on November 2, 1943. Planes from his command he reported had destroyed 55 aircraft and sunk 114,000 tons of enemy shipping there. The correct figures, according to Dr. James's researches, were 20 enemy planes shot down and 5,000 tons of Japanese shipping sent to the bottom. Just how wide of the mark he may have been in other similar communiqués no one has taken the time to reckon.

MacArthur could seldom bear to accept an adversary position when dealing face to face with anyone who owned the ability to cast even a minor blight upon the MacArthur image. In July 1950 MacArthur's stiff-necked public-relations officer, Colonel Marion Echols, almost certainly at MacArthur's behest, banned two correspondents from Korea because they had been guilty of "objectionable reporting"; they had dealt truthfully with the low level of training and equipment among the first troops to be engaged. The correspondents, Tom Lambert of Associated Press and Peter Kalischer of United Press, protested to their bureau chiefs, who then accompanied them to carry the protest to MacArthur. MacArthur, who pretended he had not even known of the ban, greeted Lambert and Kalischer as "old friends," insisted that censorship was "abhorrent" to him and, according to a report of the incident in *Time* (July 24, 1950) promptly rescinded the ban.

MacArthur's distaste for censorship had apparently developed almost overnight, for all during the occupation of Japan he had freely censored the Japanese newspapers. Richard Lauterbach, in *Danger from the East,* tells of a time when a Tokyo newspaper, *Jiji Shimpo,* wished to run an editorial warning the populace against believing that MacArthur was a living god. The MacArthur office, after a week's delay, approved the editorial for publication. But when the *Nippon Times,* an English-language newspaper read chiefly by the occupation forces applied for and received permission to reprint the editorial, the permission was suddenly withdrawn while the presses were already rolling. Charles Willoughby, MacArthur's intelligence officer, descended on the *Nippon Times* plant along with a squad of military police, ordered the presses stopped, and sent his men out to recapture all the printed copies of the paper from trains and trucks. "Occupation authorities," Willoughby declared, "must be protected from correspondents."

The dangerous thoughts in *Nippon Times* that Willoughby feared might damage the Occupation were these (quoted in Lauterbach's *Danger from the East*):

> Now a few Japanese must once have esteemed Hitler as a person greater than Napoleon. More wished that a Hitler might emerge from among the Japanese. It may be assumed that today many Japanese are wishing for General MacArthur to take the leadership of the nation.
>
> It must be emphasized that unless and until the Japanese are cleansed of this servile concept, democracy in Japan will make no progress. . . . The first step in the process of democratization must be to rid the nation of the habit of hero worship which has imbued [Japanese] minds for the past twenty centuries.

A year later, when a Japanese company set out to present Gilbert and Sullivan's *The Mikado,* long banned in Japan, SCAP ordered the production halted.

But MacArthur's office, Lauterbach reports, did not confine themselves to censoring Japanese communications. The Tokyo edition of *Stars and Stripes* was prevented from publishing a letter signed by forty-four GIs griping about the food. And two members of the GI staff were removed because of a "negative loyalty check." One had fought for the Loyalists in Spain. Another had once edited a CIO newspaper in the United States. A letter

about foreign policy addressed to President Truman by
Henry A. Wallace and the copy of a subsequent speech
were held up for forty-eight hours by the MacArthur office
and then released for publication in Tokyo so badly cut up
that they made no sense. A New Year's Day (1947) message from President Philip Murray of the CIO was also
heavily censored to eliminate all mention of labor's opposition to dictatorship and an invitation to send Japanese
delegates to the World Federation of Trade Unions. Publication of the details of the atom bombing of Hiroshima and
Nagasaki was also suppressed by the MacArthur regime
and further investigations into the results of the disaster
were forbidden.

Of course, petty duplicity of this sort and declarations of
devotion to "principle" followed by violations in practice
are endemic in political and military circles, or indeed in
any circles where a shining public countenance is of more
account than private virtue. But MacArthur often carried
his pretenses to a point where they left sores that were long
in healing. Mention has already been made of his double-
dealing with Stilwell, recorded by Dr. James, when Mac-
Arthur assured Stilwell of command of the Tenth Army
and a few days later urged appointment of another man,
with Stilwell as second choice. In Volume 2 of *The Years of
MacArthur,* Dr. James offers another example:

Dissatisfied with the progress of the attack on Buna, in
the Papuan campaign, MacArthur sent Major General
Robert Eichelberger to relieve Major General Edwin F.
Harding, commanding general of the American forces
there. He assured Harding that he had removed him only
because "anyone would be exhausted" after such a stretch
of unrelieved combat, that he should go back to Australia,
rest up, and return for a new job. Then MacArthur wrote

to Prime Minister Curtin of Australia asking that Harding's name be removed from the list of officers MacArthur had recommended for inclusion on a list to be named for prestigious British decorations. Also, once Eichelberger was in command, MacArthur sent in the reinforcements Harding had been vainly begging for through weeks of jungle fighting. And Harding was never offered that "new job."

MacArthur's dealings with General Ridgway, who had apparently awakened MacArthur's jealousy by his success with the very same forces MacArthur had found inadequate, were also marked by hypocrisy.

General Ridgway writes of his own puzzlement at two widely divergent appraisals of Ridgway as a commander. Before he left Tokyo, after turning over Supreme Command to Ridgway, MacArthur shook Ridgway's hand and told him: "If I had been permitted to choose my own successor, I'd have selected you." Three years later, he told Jim Lucas, Scripps Howard correspondent, that he rated Ridgway, "at the bottom of the list" of field commanders (Ridgway, *The Korean War*).

Yet, in a book by MacArthur's chief sycophant, Major General Courtney Whitney, it is set forth as a fact that MacArthur himself had asked to have Ridgway sent out to Korea to take over Eighth Army after Walker's death. General J. Lawton Collins, Army Chief of Staff, according to Whitney, "at first demurred but MacArthur was insistent and that evening received word that Ridgway was leaving for Tokyo at once." Compare this to the exchange that took place at a conference held at the Harry S. Truman Memorial Library in May 1975 entitled "The Korean War: A Twenty-Five Year Perspective." During the discussion, General Collins and Averell Harriman spoke of the choice of Ridgway to succeed Walker.

Said Harriman: ". . . after the trip in August 1950, General Norstad and I recommended to the President that General Walker be relieved and that General Ridgway be appointed in his place . . . and he said, 'Talk to Bradley about it' and I do not know whether Bradley . . ."

Collins responded: "No. It was not brought up before the Chiefs. However, I had talked with General MacArthur about the possibility of General Walker being killed in action . . . and I had also recommended Matt Ridgway to take over Eighth Army when and if anything happened."

That hardly resembles a "demurral." It does appear rather that MacArthur, with the assistance of his alter ego, was trying to buy a little credit for having pushed the selection of Ridgway (who turned out to be the ideal choice) and for having done so in the face of opposition from Washington. And taking credit for the accomplishments of others was one more aspect of MacArthur's uneasy nature, which required a constant flow of acclaim, recognition, high grades and victories.

MacArthur received credit in lavish measure for his accomplishments in the "democratization" of Japan, some of it deserved and much of it excessive. Certainly no other personage could have been chosen from among the victorious allies who could have slipped so naturally into the role of vice-emperor of the Japanese. No other figure in the world at that time could have combined regal bearing, autocratic manner, mystic aloofness, physical beauty, courage, and eloquence (or its like) with obvious good will and devotion to peace. MacArthur looked, behaved and carried himself like a god and indeed was accepted as one by many of the plain folk in Japan, who adored him beyond reason and swamped him with fan mail—which he did not disdain to read (after it had been duly translated and digested) for hours at a time. One wonders why he could not have let that position remain as the pinnacle of his career, instead of fantasizing, as he did, about becoming "Supreme Commander for the Defense" or United Nations Governor of Japan—or President of the United States.

The myth of MacArthur's "great success" in turning Japan into an instant democracy, like the myth of his island-hopping magic and meager casualties in the Southwest Pacific, persists in the face of a mountain of facts that modify it. There will probably never be a better book written about MacArthur's reign in Japan than Richard E. Lauterbach's *Danger from the East,* a product of industrious research and study, patient investigation, firsthand observation, thoughtful assessment, and objective judgment. In it, Lauterbach makes it painfully clear that democracy never blossomed—and could not have blossomed—overnight in Japan and that MacArthur's haste to welcome it only made its development more difficult.

Announcing victory well before it was actually in hand was a standard practice for MacArthur. He was always impatient for the trumpets. At Sanananda, he declared the battle over weeks before the fighting stopped. He announced the imminent retaking of Manila on February 6, 1945, accepted congratulations from all over the world, and planned a victory parade for February 14. It was March 6, after a mighty artillery bombardment and weeks of bitter fighting that the city was finally freed—in such a state of ruin that the victory parade was canceled. He had declared Leyte cleared of the enemy except for "minor mopping up" on Christmas 1944. But in his own story, *Jungle Road,* General Eichelberger relates:

> Actually, the Japanese army was still intact. . . . Soon Japanese began streaming across the Ormoc Valley, well-

equipped and apparently well-fed. It took several months of the roughest kind of combat to defeat this army. Between Christmas and the end of the campaign we killed 27,000 Japs.

Leyte was finally cleared of Japanese in May 1945.

And so, in hailing the return of democracy to Japan, MacArthur once more jumped the gun. Elections, he announced, were to be held on April 10, 1946—the first free elections in Japan. The Far Eastern Commission in Washington (the eleven-nation policy-making committee for Japan) protested, according to Lauterbach, that it might be too soon to expect "a fully instructed, intelligent and authoritative expression of the views of the Japanese people on their political future" and that members of the Commission had some apprehension that the holding of elections at such an early date may well give an advantage to the reactionary parties. . . ." As it turned out, these apprehensions were well founded. But MacArthur brushed them aside, with assurances that if it "proved disadvantageous" he retained the power to dissolve the Diet and call for new elections.

Lauterbach reports the elections in these words:

Both before and after the elections there were more outbursts against Premier Shidehara. Just three days prior to the balloting a large and disorderly crowd threw rocks through the windows of his home and injured eight policemen. . . . But . . . 27 million Japanese went to the polls peacefully and cast their votes for some 3000 candidates, most of whom they had never heard about before. . . .

The man who received the most votes was a tall, well-groomed man in his sixties, the President of the Liberal Party, named Ichiro Hatoyama, the former Minister of

Education who in 1932 had busied himself in suppressing progressive student movements and persecuting professors guilty of "dangerous thoughts." But he had been, like all Diet candidates, "carefully screened" by MacArthur's office. What the screening failed to bring out was the fact that Hatoyama was the author of a book titled *The Face of the World,* in which Hatoyama told of visits to Germany and Italy where he observed, and deeply admired, the works of Hitler and Mussolini. Inasmuch as MacArthur's own official censor and handyman, Colonel Willoughby, was himself a devout and vocal admirer of Hitler's dear friend, Francisco Franco, this attitude might not have troubled the MacArthur entourage as much as it did some of the Japanese. But the Japanese press hesitated to attack Hatoyama's record because they assumed (correctly) that he had been approved by SCAP. Only after Hatoyama came out on top in the voting did the story emerge and spread throughout the electorate. Soon SCAP set out to have Hatoyama declared ineligible to serve in the Diet.

Ultimately the premier's job was awarded to Shigeru Yoshida, former Japanese ambassador to Italy, who had sought and secured assurances from Mussolini of support for Japanese designs for Asia. In England, as an envoy of Hirohito, Yoshida had also staunchly defended the Japanese takeover in Manchuria. He was, obviously, no man of peace, and he carried no taint of democracy. But he had, before Japan surrendered, urged the cabinet to seek a negotiated peace and thereby earned himself a short spell in jail, enough to qualify him in the eyes of SCAP as at least not a war criminal.

The government Yoshida formed was about as far from democracy as could be conceived, short of putting power back in the hands of the shoguns. It was, according to

Asahi, Japan's leading newspaper, "closely tied to the reactionary bureauracy." Another newspaper, *Manaichi,*
quoted by Lauterbach, suggested that the new cabinet
would "probably attempt to patch up the situation without
damaging the interest of big business and the other privi-
leged classes. Without doubt this kind of government is in-
capable of solving the present crisis."

The election was remarkable, however, in that for the
first time women were allowed to vote. As a result thirty-
nine women were elected to the Diet. And the enfranchise-
ment of women was surely one of MacArthur's major con-
tributions to the growth of democracy—even though, in
practice, women remained for a long time heavily exploited
and routinely kept in subjection.

One group of women did, however, rejoice in the Mac-
Arthur reforms. They were the prostitutes who had been
routinely indentured by their families to the operators of
the whorehouses in the notorious Yoshiwara district.
Moved, they said, by the new "spirit of democracy" the
Brothel-Keepers Association in Tokyo freed the girls from
indenture and permitted them to keep half their earnings.
MacArthur quickly sanctioned this move in the name of
"fundamental human rights." One young lady who went by
the name of Plum Blossom gave thanks out loud to Mac-
Arthur and declared that the good general had "almost
doubled my earning power."

It is true that MacArthur's government in its early enthusiasm for transplanting American liberties to the vol-
canic soil of Japan did plant seeds that were bound to
flower in later years, did make converts to democratic
ideals, and ultimately provided the Japanese a far more
open society than other conquerors had brought to other
lands.

MacArthur began his job with a number of high-minded, highly skilled, and dedicated men in charge of the various sections of the Occupation. But he yielded early in the game to his reliance on his own set of sycophants. In place of Brigadier General William Crist, who had been trained for the task of running the Government Section of the Occupation and who had headed the military government in Okinawa, he named his own intimate, Courtney Whitney, thus guaranteeing that many of the democratic reforms would not last long enough to be celebrated. Courtney, a right-winger of the most rigid sort, and a practiced anti-Semite, was far more concerned with rooting out "leftists" than with spreading American-type freedoms.

One of the ablest members of the Occupation team in the first days was Brigadier General Ken R. Dyke, a New York advertising man of an extraordinarily independent cast of mind. As chairman of the Association of National Advertisers he had startled his colleagues by offering them sharp warnings on the dangers of phony advertising claims. In Tokyo Dyke was handicapped, as most members of the team were, by a failure to understand the difference between Japanese and American traditions of communication. Some of his ambitious efforts to show the Japanese, through *March of Time*-type movies, the truth about Japanese aggression, simply missed the target because the Japanese were bewildered by the hyped-up tones and the misplaced blasts of music. But Dyke worked hard to try to implant democratic ideas, through education and religion. He ordered all the Japanese histories turned to pulp so that new ones might be provided with the militarism wrung out of them. He called for a purge of the Japanese state religion of Shintoism, long a tool for implanting the theories of blind obedience and of consigning one's life to the greater glory of the Emperor. Dyke also insisted that opinions of every hue be given access to the press and radio, even the opinions of Communists. When Japanese leaders protested, Dyke told them simply: "That is what we mean by freedom of the press."

But that is not what MacArthur and Whitney meant. When Dyke left his post to return to the National Broadcasting Company as vice-president in charge of programs (where he promptly squelched the Nice-Nellieism that had kept even the word "diaper" off the air), Whitney and his minions, who had been privately calling Dyke a "pinko," quickly set about shaking out the "leftists" in Dyke's section.

To coincide with the election, MacArthur also unveiled what he must have felt was his masterpiece—the new Japanese constitution. He earnestly pretended that this instrument had been evolved through long consultation among leading Japanese minds, with SCAP holding itself studiously aloof and allowing the Diet to bring it forth fully armed from its collective forehead.

MacArthur did make an effort to impel the Japanese to write the new constitution, and he at least pretended that the work was to be done by constitutional experts selected by the Emperor, the cabinet, and the Diet. The Emperor promptly chose Prince Fumimaro Konoye, a former premier, to study the problem first. The cabinet selected a constitutional lawyer named Matsumoto for the job. Almost immediately, Konoye was named a war criminal, and before he could be arrested by occupation authorities, he committed suicide. MacArthur at once disowned Konoye, insisting he had never been cleared for the job. But newspaper correspondents were well aware that Konoye had been a favorite of SCAP.

After this disaster, the Diet set about to do the job collectively and spent months in vain discussion, with no one quite daring to father any such radical proposals as SCAP was insisting on—particularly outlawing war and stripping the Emperor of the supreme power he was supposed to be wielding. Lauterbach, in *Danger from the East,* reproduces a discussion on the subject he listened to (with an interpreter's help) in the Diet and it is almost comic in its fatuity and evasiveness.

MacArthur finally lost patience and handed the task to General Whitney, who called twenty-two members of the Government Section into secret conclave early in February 1946 and directed them to come up with a new constitution. It was his aim, he declared, to have the instrument ready for official consideration by Washington's Birthday. That meant the planners would have just ten days to complete their work. They soon discovered that the task was more complex than it seemed. But they did labor mightily, and ably, using American, British and Japanese models as guides and borrowing phraseology from the Declaration of Independence and the Gettysburg Address. And they did create a constitution well adapted to the current political trends in Japan, creating a parliamentary democracy.

But to present this composition as a Japanese creation was laughable. None of the Japanese journalists was deceived for half an instant, and they adopted a standard joke:

"Have you read the *Shinkempo* (New Constitution)?"

"No. Has it been translated into Japanese yet?"

But MacArthur would not permit the Japanese newspapers to publish such a libel. The constitution, he insisted, had grown right out of Japanese roots without his lending much more than some good advice. One scholar, Harold S.

Quigley, however, writing in the October 1947 issue of the *American Political Science Review,* flatly declared: "Obviously, no Japanese conceived or wrote the lines quoted in the new preamble. They were composed while the old constitution was in force and would have been arrant *lèse majesté* under it. . . ."

Mark Gayn, Tokyo correspondent for the *Chicago Sun,* put it more bluntly: ". . . any high school child simply by reading it [the new Constitution] can perceive its foreign origin."

Still MacArthur persisted in his fairy tale. In his *Reminiscences,* he recalls that, after he grew impatient with the inability of the Japanese Constitutional Problem Investigation Committee to come up with a document, ". . . I directed my staff to assist and advise with the Japanese in the formation of an acceptable draft. The prime minister himself [that would be Shidehara, whose windows would be broken by a mob just before the election] became active and energetic in its final preparation. . . ."

But MacArthur indulged in an even wilder flight of fancy when he tried to envision the glad acceptance of the *Shinkempo* by the "masses of the Japanese people."

It was circulated throughout Japan [MacArthur writes] and earnestly debated for a month. Ideas for small changes were forwarded from all sections, but by and large the people liked it and approved it in wholehearted fashion. The only dissenters, as might have been expected, were the Communists. The government carried out a large-scale educational program in the papers and on the radio, explaining all the features and answering questions. The April election was what I wanted, a true plebiscite. The people who had publicly committed themselves to the adoption were elected to a strong and clear majority in the new Diet.

MacArthur naturally omitted the fact that many of those who committed themselves to the adoption had done so after being assured that Article IX, outlawing war and the maintenance of land, sea and air forces was not to be taken too seriously. He also apparently had committed himself to the fable that the Japanese people were completely literate. As Lauterbach makes clear, Japanese "literacy " was partly imaginary. There are 56,000 ideographs (of Chinese origin) in the Japanese language. In primary school a student spent more than half his time learning how to read and write these symbols. By the time he graduated he had been "taught" about 1,400 and he remembered only 600, on the average. So completely was the average Japanese insulated from the "official" tongue that immediately after Hirohito's broadcast of the decision to surrender, citizens, assuming that he had proclaimed final victory, staged a joyous parade in a small town not far from Tokyo, and it lasted until the speech had been translated, on the radio, into colloquial Japanese. Even in the Diet, only about half the members understood what the Emperor was saying.

To understand a newspaper completely, a Japanese needs to know 2,400 characters. And unless he has a grasp of some 10,000 characters he cannot read and understand a college textbook. As in other ancient cultures, the written language was retained through the centuries as a barrier between the plain people and all knowledge of what their rulers were contriving among themselves. And in Japan under MacArthur, despite the efforts of American authorities who recognized the problem, the upper classes prevented the adoption of the Roman alphabet, or any variation of it—even though experiments illustrated that children could learn in two weeks what it took them six years to learn in studying the old-style characters.

Although MacArthur certainly must have awakened at some point to the fact that all was not going well with his program of democratization and land reform or with his efforts to break up the great industrial combines that had grown fat on Japan's military conquests, he records no hint of this in his *Reminiscences*. It was not MacArthur's sole fault by any means that the Occupation did not succeed either in doing away with the *Zaibatsu* (money clique that had managed the entire nation, including the Emperor), in changing the content of Japanese education, stamping out militarism or eradicating landlordism. The Japanese, seeing many of the reforms coming, sought out devious inventions to evade them—turning farmer-tenants into farmer-employers, for instance, so that the land would seem to be owned by the person who "worked" it, setting up Control Associations to replace *Zaibatsu* monopolistic practices with similar practices under "government control," and persuading GIs (who were not limited in the amount of money they could exchange) to convert "old" yen into "new," so that many Japanese, now that bank accounts were officially frozen, could still get their hands on far more cash than they were allowed.

SCAP simply did not have manpower enough to enforce the reform provisions, and much of the manpower they did have was busy, not looking for evasions of land-reform and industrial-production rules, but ferreting out hidden stores of arms and other illegal treasures. Besides, MacArthur and those who acted for him were handicapped in Japan, as later in Korea, in making moves that might seem to be anti-free-enterprise. To have permitted industrial plants or transportation or communications to be put into the hands of employees, or "nationalized" in any way that denied profits to investors, would have been promptly damned, at home and in Japan, as rank socialism.

So MacArthur, in recording his dealings in all these matters, recalls one "triumph" after another. His "interpretation" of the antiwar section of the new constitution was prompt, ensuring that the restriction on armed forces would not apply "should the course of world events require that all mankind stand to arms in defense of human liberty." Inasmuch as every war in which the United States took up arms had been "in defense of human liberty" of one sort or another, this interpretation made it clear that Japan might rearm itself if it chose to fight on our side.

All this is not to say, of course, that the new constitution was not a blessing to Japan. Nor did it need to be forced down Japanese throats. Democracy was really not a mystery to the Japanese, although many were bewildered by MacArthur's dictatorial moves in the name of "democracy," just as North Korea had a hard time identifying the democratic component in Communist rule. Japan was not a counterpart of Italy and Germany nor was Hirohito, despite United States wartime propaganda, an Oriental Hitler or Mussolini. The apparatus for democracy—popular elections and an elected legislature—still existed, despite the fact that the shoguns of the industrial-military clique manipulated the Emperor while reactionaries controlled the Diet. Even in our own democracy, like situations have sometimes been envisioned by some of our leaders.

The major reforms wrought through the constitution and the Government Section of the Occupation were all accomplished with MacArthur's blessing—and without too much foresight. The able men and women, largely anonymous now, who helped devise them for the Japanese to implement, were able to work almost immune from the pressure to compromise or distort, and so they included liberties that even the United States had not yet enjoyed in

an unalloyed state. (The "equal-rights amendment" for
women was adopted in Japan when it had barely taken
form at home.) As Edwin O. Reischauer has pointed out in
The Japanese, revolutionary reforms "are easier and more
fun in someone else's country."

Surely there could have been far worse Supreme Commanders in charge of the remaking of democracy in Japan.
Admiral William F. "Bull" Halsey, for instance, who
wanted to "kick all the Japs in the face." Or Dean Acheson, who, at least in the early days of the Occupation, was
all for stamping out the military spirit in Japan with an
iron heel, or Henry Morgenthau, who no doubt would have
wanted Japanese industry razed to the ground as he had
wanted to destroy Germany's.

MacArthur, however, seemed to relish the role of a man
of peace. Descending from his plane at Atsugi Air Base
that summer morning in 1945, carrying no arms more lethal than his enormous corncob pipe, he soon symbolized
to the Japanese all that was magnanimous and peace-lov-
ing in the American character. His grand gestures and re-
sounding abstractions well suited his role as a sort of living
statue. And his own great sense of theater prompted him to
seize eagerly upon some of the reforms submitted to him
by the people who were formulating the new laws that the
Japanese were to live by. Undoubtedly he relished the vision of himself as he struck the bonds from the limbs of
tenant farmers and indentured prostitutes. His guaranteeing the rights of labor (a move he soon regretted) enabled him to picture himself as labor's choice for President
at home. His helping women cast off their own shackles no
doubt suited the promptings of his own heart. But his
commitment to destroying the combines of the "Mer-
chants of Death"—the *Zaibatsu* that controlled all industry—was another move he probably wished he had never

endorsed, for he soon found himself assailed by many of the "better people" at home, those wealthy businessmen who, he had no doubt been taught, represented all that was able and sound in America.

Trying to dismember that military-industrial complex in Japan while still protecting "free enterprise" was a wearying task anyway, with the reactionaries in full control of the Diet and with even the men who had been purged from high positions in industry still exerting influence through friends and close associations. By the time MacArthur was about a quarter way through the job, the cries of "socialism" had grown too intense to ignore, and the economy had begun to wobble so that MacArthur was already talking out loud about having the United Nations take over the job of setting the clock ahead in Japan.

The labor unions had reacted with frenzy to the sudden freeing of their leaders from jail and the promulgation of guarantees of their rights to organize, to bargain collectively, and to strike. Inflation had already left wages so far behind that even a 200 percent increase in wage rates would not have evened matters up. Railroad workers were among the most innovative strikers. When their demands were flatly rejected by management, they declared a "strike" that did not include their leaving their jobs. As Lauterbach describes the event, the railroad workers, who were asking for a 500 percent increase, kept operating the trains, but began collecting much higher fares from the passengers. With the extra money they first paid themselves the wages they wanted and put the leftovers in escrow for management. They also accomplished a spectacular increase in productivity at the repair shops. With the union itself directing operations, the shops began to overhaul fifteen cars a day, ten times what the shops had been able to turn out before. So management met the wage demands and the strike was ended.

This method of "production control" put a scare into some State Department figures, for it smelled very strongly of a socialistic, even communistic, practice, particularly when municipal employees in Tokyo took over running of the city government and did a much better job of it than the politicians had done. The Yoshida government opposed this innovation, and MacArthur himself began to make outspoken attacks on the labor movement, culminating in his forbidding a general strike—which perhaps would have wrecked the functioning of the Occupation completely—and his identifying his stand as "anti-Communist." From then on the government too used the Communist label to darken, in the eyes of MacArthur, every labor action. Eventually MacArthur MPs even found themselves breaking up picket lines, while MacArthur's chief Communist-hunter, Charles Willoughby, known to junior officers as "Prince Charles," concentrated on rooting leftists out of the unions.

While the transfer of farmland to the folk who tilled it did not work out exactly as the reformers hoped, a great sweep of land was taken for transfer to former tenants by the government, and paid for at preinflation prices, that amounted to plain confiscation. The law that limited farmland ownership to 7.5 acres kept the well-to-do from monopolizing choice acreage. Despite dire predictions, farm production soared under the new system, although it was a long time before there was a true sufficiency of food grown in Japan.

The reform that may have helped most in rebuilding the economy and put a definite brake on the reestablishment of the money cliques, the *Zaibatsu,* was the new tax system, designed by Professor Carl Shoup of Columbia University. Professor Shoup had been recruited for the job by Lon Harold Moss of the Bureau of Internal Revenue, who was sent to Tokyo at the special request of General MacArthur. MacArthur, on November 1, 1947, had written to George Schoeneman, the Commissioner of Internal Revenue, and specifically asked to have Moss assigned to Tokyo, so MacArthur must receive some of the credit, or blame, for the result. Had he been less naïve about matters of economics and finance, perhaps MacArthur would have thought twice about the possible event of this assignment.

As it turned out, Shoup was given a free hand, even allowed to choose his own colleagues—all from academic circles—and come in his own good time, which was spring 1948. And he insisted that his report, when it was made, be published in both English and Japanese, so that native Japanese would not have to have the results explained to them. MacArthur agreed to that too. Shoup and his team, unlike some other MacArthur minions, did not scorn to move out among the plain people, to the farm country, into the factories, even down into the coal mines. Uneasy about the worsening state of the economy, MacArthur and the Japanese both gave Shoup intense cooperation—interpreters, transportation, protection from the special pleaders, access to every source of information. All MacArthur asked was that *some* sort of income-tax system be devised before the roof fell in.

What Shoup came up with was, he said recently, except for the abolition of the sales tax, not a revolutionary reform. It was a radical improvement in administration that left fewer loopholes to pull fat profits through, that relied on the individual to figure out and remit his own taxes, thus putting an end to the system of farming out taxes to collectors, and that updated depreciation formulas so corporate profits could no longer be so easily concealed. It was this system, rather than any purging and splitting-up of the money cliques, that helped prevent the *Zaibatsu* from rising again and encouraged the growth of small business. But it was a system that could not even have got past the front door of the United States Senate. And it was the sort of system that MacArthur himself, in his campaign for the Presidency, vigorously decried as the source of all our woes and the first step on the road to Communism.

One of the most ludicrous roles that MacArthur assumed was that of Bringer of the Word to the heathen Japanese. Convinced, as he and all his courtiers were, that he had, from his time in the Far East, developed a consummate understanding of the "Oriental mind," MacArthur early in the game declared that Japan was a fertile ground for Christianity to take root in and flourish. Saint Francis Xavier having preceded MacArthur by some four hundred years, Christianity was not unknown in Japan. It had been brutally suppressed for two centuries, but in 1873 it had been permitted to resume its proselytizing—with only moderate success. By the time MacArthur appeared, practicing Christians numbered less than 1 percent of the population. Among the well-to-do and better-educated, its proportion was higher and, of course, its influence was stronger than if it had been, as it was in the beginning, the faith of the poor. Christmas, in the big Japanese cities, has long been widely and ostentatiously celebrated, as it is in New York, with minor emphasis on its religious content.

But MacArthur saw Christianity as a means of "civilizing" the Japanese, turning them to peaceful ways, and rendering them immune to "atheistic Communism." In his

Reminiscences he declares that he told Christian ministers, "The more missionaries we can bring out here and the
more occupation troops we can send home the better." He
invited the Pocket Testament League to distribute Bibles,
and he proudly records that ten million Bibles, translated
into Japanese, were placed in eager Oriental hands. "Gradually," he writes, "a spiritual regeneration in Japan began
to grow." It was gradual indeed, for the increase in the
number of Christians was minuscule. Young people in
Japan, after the war, like their counterparts in the West,
went awhoring after the strange gods of cultism while
many old folks clung to their familiar superstitions, which
they found more soul-satisfying than any ritualized liturgy.

MacArthur also proclaimed victories in reforming the
educational system, in revising textbooks, in decentralizing
the police, and in remaking the economy, hailing each as a
personal triumph, leaving the mopping-up to be done by
the nameless functionaries in the Government Section. He
did, in his book, share credit with many who headed the
various sections but along with such doughty performers
as Lon Moss, Carl Shoup, and Charles Kades (who labored
hardest on the constitution) he features the insufferable
Whitney, the jolly and ineffectual Major General William
Marquat, who admitted he knew nothing of economics, although that was the section given to his charge, and the
imperious Willoughby, whose interest in democracy was
minimal. No mention of Colonel Charles Kramer, who first
tackled the job of dismembering the *Zaibatsu,* of Ken
Dyke, who moved so forcefully and diligently to reform the
educational system, nor of Ms. Beate Sirota, who moth-
ered the women's-rights article in the constitution and
drafted clauses on civil rights. (See Dr. John Curtis Perry's
excellent book *Beneath the Eagle's Wings.*) They were

not regular Army, not members of the Bataan gang, had not been recruited by MacArthur, and may even have been too leftist to deserve notice.

Many of the reforms sponsored by the Occupation fell far short of the immediate goal or simply would not work. The educational reform by purging the militaristic personnel left the schools short of qualified teachers; there were not enough teachers who had not been thoroughly brainwashed or intimidated. Alterations in the history books were often more cosmetic than substantive. Decentralizing the police put too heavy a financial burden on small communities, and the project had to be abandoned.

Yet the Occupation was at least a partial success, thanks largely to the Japanese themselves, who needed not so much a reeducation along American lines as freedom from the yoke of militarism and brutal exploitation. After that, the mysterious Oriental mind turned out to be much like the Western mind—at least in its understanding of which side of the bread wore the butter and its preoccupation with brass-tacks realities. *Time* (March 24, 1947) told the story of Shiro Suzuki, a twenty-year-old ex-soldier who had been drifting about Tokyo, sleeping in railroad stations, waiting for his chance to take an examination for entrance to the university. Suzuki spoke for "his fellow students":

We students talk and talk but cannot find the answers. . . . In Japan today there are many restrictions which MacArthur has placed upon the people which are not the will of the people. Where is the difference between democracy and what we had before the war?

I don't know. There are too many things about democracy which we students have not the time to study. All of us here walk three kilometers a day to get a meal or a little rice and radish. It is difficult to contemplate the philosophy of government under such circumstances.

The government also eventually found a loophole that permitted it to finance private schools, despite a statutory prohibition of such practice under MacArthur's Occupation. And, by the time the American forces finally did go home, the central government had regained its hold on the public schools and began to introduce, not the old-time "morals," or *kokutai,* the "Die for duty" precept of prewar Japan, but a form of "ethics" so much like it that some students could not see the difference. One twenty-year-old student, quoted in *Japan Today* (1970s) by William Forbis, said of the new doctrine: "The kind of moral education enforced by the state is designed to create characterless people who are obedient to the Establishment."

And while MacArthur deplored the tendency of Japanese labor unions to establish political goals, labor was not to be misled into believing that the Yoshida government was anything but the bitter enemy of the wage earners and they went their militant way, becoming gradually estranged from the Occupation, until wage scales eventually created their own thriving consumer market for Japanese goods, right inside Japan. And finally the Korean War, which turned Japan into a booming arsenal and army camp beyond the sound of angry guns, started wheels turning, and ships and plants abuilding, and fresh troops athronging, and cash flowing as never before.

Of course the promulgation of the Truman Doctrine, changing the mission of the Occupation force from building democracy in Japan to creating there a mighty bulwark against Communism, turned MacArthur's job from a monumental task into an impossible one. Still, MacArthur, despite his surpassing ability to maintain the pose of the magnanimous conqueror and Man of Peace—a role he must have dearly loved—was not by any means the right person to spread the doctrine of democracy. He had no real understanding of democracy himself nor much experience of it, having lived most of his life by the rules of the Army caste system. He believed devoutly in the natural superiority of the well-to-do and the well-educated and was entirely comfortable with the fiercely antidemocratic natures of folk like Syngman Rhee, Chiang Kai-shek, Shigeru Yoshida and Manuel Roxas. His own closest friends and most intimate associates were all men of decidedly antidemocratic views. Almost all flaunted strong prejudices and some were openly racist.

Clark Lee, one of MacArthur's consistently admiring biographers, wrote of MacArthur's "complete absence of any racial prejudice." William Manchester, by no means a worshipful biographer, reports that MacArthur's aide and interpreter, Major Faubion Bowers, wrote that MacArthur once referred to President Roosevelt as "Rosenfeld," spoke of Truman as "that Jew in the White House," and pointed out that Truman's name and features were Jewish—with the obvious implication that there was something shameful about this. Manchester, however, offers in mitigation the allegation that Eleanor Roosevelt and Adlai Stevenson were equally guilty of "benign anti-Semitism" of this sort "in their early years." But these were not MacArthur's early years. Nor was there anything benign—if there ever could be—about the anti-Semitism preached by some of MacArthur's close associates. While MacArthur may in truth have been free of racism, he surely had a fine tolerance for it.

MacArthur was an honorary member of the Southern Society in New York, an organization that, you may be sure, was not open to blacks. Of the four swimming pools in Tokyo available to troops during the Occupation, three were declared "off limits" to blacks. When President Truman issued an executive order requiring the integration of black troops into white units, MacArthur refused to conform. Despite the fact that the all-black 24th Infantry fought gallantly and successfully in the first Allied offensive action in Korea, the sixteen-hour battle for Yuchon, United States troops were not integrated until General Ridgway took over as supreme commander.

Lieutenant General Edward Almond, MacArthur's Chief of Staff and obvious favorite, who had commanded an all-black infantry division in World War II, was the author of a top-secret report on the "combat efficiency" of black troops. In November 1947, he sent a copy of this report to Major General A. V. Arnold, who had requested it, and explained in a covering letter that the report

> ought to be carefully guarded and not quoted except in abstract, eliminating reference to the designation of units and names of individuals concerned whether white or colored. The very nature of the reports, if bandied around in the press, particularly the colored press, would defeat the purpose for which it is intended.

Almond then explained:

> In my opinion, a large negro organization, with a good stiffening of white officers in command in high staff positions will be excellent from the line of the regimental CP's towards the rear, that is, in supply and artillery aspects and will be poor to zero forward of that line.

In January 1948, Almond in another letter to Arnold, told him:

It is my earnest hope that it [the report] may prove of value in our future mobilization and training and constitute a document of fact and not fancy or hope that will serve as a guide to those who may need help in utilizing negroes in accordance with their capabilities.

Major General Courtney Whitney, MacArthur's most intimate associate, and the only one of his staff who was allowed to walk unannounced into the spacious office in the Dai Ichi building where MacArthur concealed himself, made no secret of his anti-Semitism, which would hardly have been termed "benign," nor is it possible that it could have been unobserved by MacArthur. Once, when Whitney sat with a group of strangers in the smoking compartment of a New York-to-Washington Pullman, there was talk about MacArthur in which one traveler, an ex-Navy man, offered a belittling comment about Whitney's boss— without knowing of course just what Whitney's connection was. After eliciting an unexpectedly angry rejoinder, the man who made the remark left the compartment. Whitney, his eyes still ablaze, turned to those remaining. "He must be a *kike!*" he cried. Jews, one had to assume, were the natural enemies of MacArthur.

This was certainly the doctrine of another of MacArthur's oldest and most trusted friends, Major General George Van Horn Moseley, who served as MacArthur's Deputy during MacArthur's term as Army Chief of Staff. In 1943, when MacArthur's ambition to become President first began to stir, Moseley, self-appointed political adviser, wrote MacArthur warning him that the "Jews and un-

Americans are hoping that the President [Franklin Roosevelt] may run; but they are taking no chances. I understand they are supporting Willkie with all kinds of money, so that if he should be elected they will still be in the saddle. In my opinion Willkie has turned out to be a contemptible individual. When he was first discovered, everyone felt, I believe, that an able, honest business man had been found. Then he sold out to the vicious elements now in control. . . ."

Moseley invariably lumped Jews and un-Americans together, as he did "labor and communists." MacArthur's response to this letter was that it contained "much food for thought."

On October 15, 1945, Moseley wrote MacArthur again about "conditions throughout the United States." "There are," Moseley wrote,

a great many enemies within our gates who, while they must admire you secretly, they are afraid of you officially. Among this number are the members of the C.I.O., The Communists and Jews and such skunks as Walter Winchell and Drew Pearson. You would be amazed at the control these undesirable individuals have in the press and in the movies. Combined, they have put out of business some of our most loyal publications, or where they have not actually put them out of business, they have bought them out, changed the directing personnel and the policy of the paper. You must understand these groups are doing everything they dare to smear you. They fear, I believe, that something might bring you back to America with the mission to clean house in America from coast to coast, and Lord knows we need it. As I once pointed out, there are just about enough telegraph poles from the Atlantic to the Pacific to accommodate all these rascals.

The Jews are making the same mistake that they have always made before being thrown out of the country in which they were domiciled. Today throughout America they are doing just what they did in Germany, that is, buying up everything they can. The plan seems to be to get possession of everything they can, then depreciate our currency, and pay off all their mortgages and bills in worthless dollars, leaving them in possession with no mortgages whatsoever. Our people are beginning to realize this very generally, and while Hitler has few friends in the United States, one hears on all sides today that Hitler was right in one thing he did— and that is, in getting rid of the Jews. . . .

The sad picture today is to see American manpower as it appears on Main Street throughout the land. In many cities, it is a sad sight. This fair city of Atlanta is being taken over by the Jews lock, stock and barrel. Tney have occupied Peachtree Street completely. It is a sad commentary in America today that if one investigates the dope traffic, the red light district, the liquor traffic, the black market, rotten literature, printed for our youngsters to read, he runs head on into a pack of Jews. If you read this letter to this point, please do not say that George Moseley is cracked on the subject of the Jews, for I am not. I have studied them carefully, and I know their plans. The thing that provokes me is to witness the way the Jew is executing his plans and playing the Christian as a sucker. They are preaching tolerance to the Gentiles all over the States where there is no tolerance in their own souls. Sometime ago they sent a man named Maurice Samuel over the country to lecture on this subject. Christians, in large numbers, listened to him. But this same man, Samuel, wrote a book entitled "You Gentiles." Here is a passage from that book: "We Jews, we, the destroyers, will remain the destroyers forever. Nothing that you do will meet our needs and demands. We will forever destroy because we need a world of our own." At the outbreak of the present war, a Rabbi in the West made the statement that it was too bad that war had broken out again, and that Christians would stand out and shoot Christians, but he added—"What better plan is there for us?"

If MacArthur was in any way repelled by this garbage, he had many opportunities to indicate his revulsion. But Moseley continued to ply him with political advice. In October 1947, he opened a letter to MacArthur with these words:

> Recently I was made very happy in receiving a message from "Chip" Robert that he had seen you and that you had asked to be remembered to me. When Wright Bryan of the Atlanta Journal returned, he told me you had asked after me. . . . There is only one course for you to follow remembering that with all your accomplishments to date you are a far greater character than any president. KEEP CLEAR OF ALL OFFERS AND OF ALL POLITICS. . . . Your only chance is to carry the convention by storm at that critical moment when the leading contenders are about in an even balance in the voting. . . .

Then, on May 24, 1950, Moseley wrote this in a letter to MacArthur:

> Your devoted friend of Ft. Worth, Texas and Natchez, Miss., Judge George W. Armstrong, asked me to send you a copy of his last book. You will notice that the opinions expressed are almost entirely from quoted documents. Nothing can shake Judge Armstrong's (and my) faith in you. He writes "The salvation of our country depends on him."

The book mentioned was *The Zionists,* undated, and obviously printed at the Judge's expense. These are a few of the Judge's least rabid convictions, as expressed in the book:

> . . . I allege [in a "Petition" addressed to the President and the Congress of the United States] upon information and be-

lief that Herbert H. Lehman, Felix Frankfurter and several other Congressmen and other officials are Zionist communists and *citizens of the state of Israeli* [sic].

It was revealed by Major Geo. R. Jordan that Harry Hopkins* supplied the bolsheviks with our atomic bomb blueprints and secrets, and with material for making them.... These revelations appear to be authentic. If true, they are conclusive evidence that Roosevelt was a traitor.

Zionists are all traitors; they are taught treachery by their Talmud and Protocols.

Congress should establish a tribunal for the war trials of communists.... Membership in the B'Nai B'Rith should be prima facie evidence of guilt....

Is Harry Solomon Truman Also A Traitor [Chapter heading]? ... He looks like a Jew and acts like a Zionist and consorts with Zionists and advocates the program of the Zionist Jews.

It would hardly be unfair to expect any man who had, as William Manchester declared, "scorned the racial chauvinism of ultra-rightists all his life" to consign lunatic babblings of this sort either to the garbage can or to the fire. But MacArthur found a place for it on his bookshelf. How much of it he read, who can say? The book is one of the few "authorities" for the assertion that Harry Truman's name was Jewish, that he looked like a Jew, as MacArthur was supposed to have charged, and might well have been Jewish. And there is certainly no basis for assuming that MacArthur meant such an assertion, if he uttered it, to convey approval or admiration. The book can still be found in the MacArthur library in Norfolk, where the City of Norfolk maintains its MacArthur Memorial and where it is doubtful that anyone any longer considers it "food for thought." Nor is it unfair to note the fact that there was not a sin-

* Said to have been a Zionist Jew whose real name was Harry L. Raschid.

gle member of MacArthur's inner circle who could be
identified as broad-minded on the matter of race. The third
man closest to MacArthur was Charles Willoughby, his
German-born intelligence chief. And Willoughby made it
clear to anyone who would listen that, next to MacArthur,
he deeply admired Francisco Franco as a leader and a soldier, perhaps the second-greatest who ever lived. Whether
his admiration extended to Franco's dear friend, ally, and
role-model, and Willoughby's own fellow countryman,
Adolf Hitler, is too late to discover. But it at least seems
not unlikely.

How was it then that MacArthur ever earned a reputation as a liberal as well as a Liberator? When required at
last to step down from his pedestal, discard his role as
semideity, and finally articulate his real convictions, in his
"campaign" of 1951, he revealed himself as a mediocre,
long-winded, and strident political hack out of another
century, who proposed to repeal the income-tax amendment, cancel out all other such "socialist" policies, and
save us all from "economic incompetence" by putting Big
Business back in the saddle. Even in his *Reminiscences,*
completed in 1964, he continued to assail the "Marxist-in-
spired" Federal Income Tax Law of 1914, the "process of
controlling economic conditions" and the government's
"incessant encroachment upon the capitalistic system."

Happily, the voters, even including many thousands who
had rendered him a near-hysterical welcome home, recognized the hand of Herbert Hoover behind the voice of Mac-
Arthur and refrained from offering him the kingly crown
that his fond admirers thought lay in his grasp. Like an
actor who had played a role so long that he began to believe it was his person rather than the play that had drawn
the accolades, he struggled through his tour, apparently
unknowing.

A cabal of enraptured oil millionaires financed a trip to Texas for MacArthur in a chartered Eastern Airlines plane. While there he received a brand-new Cadillac as a gift from the Houston Elks and was greeted with a 17-gun salute from artillerymen hired by Glenn McCarthy, owner of the new Shamrock Hotel, who had the salute repeated next day, when Houston business closed at four o'clock to greet the General. But crowds who came to listen to his dire warnings of imminent socialism were dwindling, with the Cotton Bowl in Dallas only one third full. Still MacArthur marched on as if the cheers were as loud as ever.

Certainly he never realized that the lines others had suggested to him, the great deeds others had designed for him, the victories men had won in his name, had never been fathered by his single self. No one ever told him that his eloquence often grew empty, frequently became choked with redundancies, and was sometimes ungrammatical. And he clung to the very end to the hope that by some magic the Republican convention might suddenly stampede for MacArthur.

Alas, there was never any basis for hope. There were, however, lesser honors. A candy firm offered to create a "MacArthur" bar—an offer he did not acknowledge—and organized baseball asked him to become Commissioner—an honor he declined.

He might better have rested content with the halo fashioned him by Representative Dewey Short who cried out, after MacArthur had addressed a joint session of Congress: "We heard God speak today! God in the flesh! The voice of God!"

acknowledgments

This book could not have been written had it not been for the untiring advice and generous help offered by one of the nation's greatest military heroes, General Matthew B. Ridgway, in seeking out sources and securing interviews. Despite the fact that his own assessment of General MacArthur differs sharply at many points from my own, he nevertheless allowed me my differences and supported my desire to find public utterance for my own conclusions.

Almost equally patient in providing answers to questions and generous in allotting me hours of his time was Colonel Johnny Austin, former Secretary to the General Staff of I Corps, Eighth Army.

Dr. Richard J. Sommers, Librarian-Archivist at the U.S. Army Military History Institute, extended his cooperation in ferreting out both rich and obscure sources far beyond the call of duty. His exceptionally competent assistants, Dr. Wesley M. Laing and Ms. Valerie Metzler, were equally patient and cooperative.

Others who offered generous assistance, despite their unwillingness to share my point of view in all particulars, were: Major General Leven C. Allen (U.S.A. ret.), Admiral Ho Keun Chang, of the ROK Navy , Dr. Sangyong Choi, Lieutenant General John A. Dabney (U.S.A. ret.), the late Vice-Admiral James H. Doyle, General Paul L. Freeman, Jr. (U.S.A. ret.), the Honorable W. Averell Harriman, Colonel Robert D. Heinl, Jr. (U.S.M.C. ret.), Bo Youp Hwang, Hae Ok Hwang, Suk Jo Kim, General J. H. Michaelis (U.S.A. ret.), Major General Frank W. Moorman (U.S.A. ret.), Honorable John Muccio, Colonel Russel P. Reeder, Jr. (U.S.A. ret.), Professor Carl Shoup, the late General Oliver P. Smith, U.S.M.C, Brigadier General Walter F. Winton, Jr. (U.S.A. ret.), and Major General Edwin K. Wright (U.S.A. ret.).

Dr. D. Clayton James provided some sage advice. Theodore Cowhig, who served in the ranks in Korea, contributed a number of vivid details. My wife, Jean, my son Robert S., and my daughters, Pam and Nora, helped sustain me throughout my labors. My daughter-in-law, Dian, discovered some valuable sources. My friend Ilona von Karolyi provided timely encouragement. My former wife, Janet W. Smith, the historian, graciously allowed me to borrow from her files.

My researches were aided nobly by the staff of the Lenox (Mass.) Library, notably Mrs. Vega Stevens, who helped locate desired volumes, and Mrs. Phyllis Ford Linstead, who proved unfailingly helpful. But all the others—Mrs. Margaret M. Kennard, Miss Sherry Gaherty, Mrs. Margaretta Keith, and Mrs. Peggy Shaftoe—contributed in large measure to the smooth functioning of this really remarkable facility.

My granddaughter, Sherry Short, helped gather up an enormous amount of material. Mike Miller at the National Archives ran down some hard-to-find documents.

As usual, the Boston Atheneum proved an ideal place to study in, and Mr. Donald Kelley of the Atheneum staff offered untiring and uncomplaining assistance in digging out needed periodicals.

Congressman Silvio Conte and his staff gave generously of their time.

George Rowe, Jr., Marshall M. Austin and Thomas W. Evans, all provided special information about engagements involving the Marine Corps.

The MacArthur Memorial in Norfolk, Virginia, was most generous in supplying copies of important documents and records.

Four excerpts from *Time* magazine have been reprinted by permission.

ROBERT SMITH

Lenox, Massachusetts
Summer 1981

bibliography

The truly definitive and authoritative biography of Douglas MacArthur is *The MacArthur Years,* a three-volume work by Dr. D. Clayton James, the third volume of which is still in progress as I write this. For objectivity, painstaking accuracy, shrewd assessment, clarity and readability, this work will probably never be matched, founded as it is on personal interviews with so many of MacArthur's contemporaries, including colleagues, superiors, subordinates, admirers, foes, and intimate friends.

For an understanding of Korean politics, no volume at present excels the beautifully written and inclusive survey by Gregory Henderson, *Korea: The Politics of the Vortex.*

First choice of volumes covering MacArthur's "reign" in occupied Japan is Richard E. Lauterbach's *Danger from the East,* a lively, anecdotal, and ringingly authoritative product of firsthand observation and personal interviews.

The story of the Inchon invasion, Operation Chromite, is brilliantly recorded in day-to-day fashion, with a strong narrative sweep, in *Victory at High Tide* by Robert Debs Heinl, Jr.

E. Grant Meade's *American Military Government in Korea* is indispensable to an understanding of what went wrong with our occupation there.

Other useful volumes are:

Acheson, Dean, *Present at the Creation,* New York, 1969.
Appleman, Roy E., *South to the Naktong, North to the Yalu,* Washington, 1961.
Baldwin, Frank, ed., *Without Parallel,* New York, 1974.

Brodie, Bernard, *War and Politics,* New York, 1973.

Dille, John, *Substitute for Victory,* New York, 1954.

Donovan, Robert J., *Conflict and Crisis,* New York, 1977.

Douglas, William O., *The Court Years,* New York, 1980.

Forbis, William H., *Japan Today,* New York, 1975.

Grajdanzev, Andrew J., *Modern Korea,* New York, 1944.

Gunther, John, *The Riddle of MacArthur,* New York, 1951.

Heller, Francis H., ed., *The Korean War: A 25-Year Perspective,* Lawrence, Kansas, 1977.

Higgins, Marguerite, *War in Korea,* New York, 1951.

Higgins, Trumbull, *Korea and the Fall of MacArthur,* New York, 1960.

Hunt, Frazier, *The Untold Story of General MacArthur,* New York, 1944.

Kelley, Frank R., and Ryan, Cornelius, *MacArthur, Man of Destiny,* New York, 1950.

Kolka, Joyce and Gabriel, *The Limits of Power: The World and U.S. Foreign Policy, 1945–54,* New York, 1972.

Kenney, George C., *The MacArthur I Know,* New York, 1951.

Leckie, Robert, *Conflict: The History of the Korean War,* New York, 1962.

Lee, Clark, and Henschel, Richard, *Douglas MacArthur,* New York, 1952.

Luvaas, Jay, ed., *Dear Miss Em,* Westport (Conn.), 1972.

MacArthur, Douglas, *Reminiscences,* New York, 1964.

Manchester, William, *American Caesar,* Boston, 1978.

Marshall, S.L.A., *The River and the Gauntlet,* New York, 1953.

McCune, George A., *Korea Today,* Cambridge, 1950.

Miller, Lynn, and Fruessen, Ronald, *Reflections on the Cold War: A Quarter Century of American Foreign Policy,* Philadelphia, 1974.

Miller, Merle, *Plain Speaking,* New York, 1973.

Morison, Samuel Eliot, *The Two-Ocean War,* Boston, 1963.

Oliver, Robert T., *Why War Came to Korea,* New York, 1950.

Perry, John Curtis, *Beneath the Eagle's Wings,* New York, 1980.

Reischauer, Edwin O., *The Japanese,* Cambridge, 1977.

Ridgway, Matthew B., *The Korean War,* Garden City, 1967.

Rovere, Richard H., and Schlesinger, Arthur M., *The General and the President, and the Future of American Foreign Policy,* New York, 1951.

Schnabel, James F., *U.S. Army in the Korean War: Policy and Direction, The First Year,* Washington, 1972.

Spanier, John W., *The Truman-MacArthur Controversy and the Korean War,* Cambridge, 1959.

Stone, I. F., *The Hidden History of the Korean War,* New York, 1952.

Truman, Harry S., *Years of Trial and Hope,* New York, 1956.

Walters, Vernon A., *Silent Missions,* Garden City, 1978.

Whitney, Courtney, *MacArthur: His Rendezvous with History,* New York, 1955.

Willoughby, Charles A., and Chamberlain, John, *MacArthur 1941-1951,* New York, 1954.

ARCHIVAL SOURCES

MacArthur Memorial, Norfolk, Virginia
    Record Group 1, Ma to PC, Box 1
    Record Group 5, SCAP, Military Secretary Correspondence
    Record Group 6, FECOM, General Correspondence
    Record Group 7, VIP File
    Record Group 9, Messages JCS. Messages, 24th Corps
    Record Group 10, VIP File
National Archives, Suitland, Maryland
    Record Group 165, Records of War Department and Special Staffs, Civil Affairs Division, 1943–49
    Record Group 218, Records of JCS, 1942–43
    Record Group 338, Messages, Correspondence
United States Army Military History Institute, Carlisle Barracks, Pa.

Edward M. Almond Collection, Correspondence, Diary, Oral History.

Hagdon A. Boatner file, correspondence

Frank H. Britton file, correspondence, documents, diary.

Richard O. Flackenstein file, correspondence.

John Hodge file, messages, correspondence.

Robert A. Howes file, diary.

William H. Quinn file, correspondence.

Matthew B. Ridgway Collection, messages, correspondence, notes, documents, oral history.

Arthur G. Trudeau file, messages, correspondence.

Orlando Ward file, messages, correspondence.

index

(Note: The initials "DM" indicate "Douglas MacArthur" throughout.)